Mississippi Writers Talking

Mississippi

Writers Talking

INTERVIEWS WITH

Eudora Welty

Shelby Foote

Elizabeth Spencer

Barry Hannah

Beth Henley

John Griffin Jones
Interviewer and Editor

UNIVERSITY PRESS OF MISSISSIPPI / JACKSON

6/1984
Am. Lit.

This volume is sponsored by the Department of Archives and History

Elbert R. Hilliard, *Director*
Charlotte Capers, *Executive Editor*

Library of Congress Cataloging in Publication Data

Main entry under title:
Mississippi writers talking.

  "Sponsored by the Department of Archives
and History"—T.p. verso.
  1. Authors, American—Mississippi—Inter-
views. 2. Authors, American—20th century—
Interviews. 3. American fiction—20th century
—History and criticism—Addresses, essays,
lectures. 4. Mississippi—Social life and
customs—Addresses, essays, lectures.
I. Jones, John G. II. Welty, Eudora, 1909–
III. Mississippi. Dept of Archives and History.
PS266.M7M5   810'.9'9762   81-23057
ISBN 0-87805-154-6 (pbk.)   AACR2
ISBN 0-87805-155-4

Contents

Foreword

John Jones joined the staff of the Mississippi Department of Archives and History in 1979. Two years later he had tape recorded interviews with eleven of America's important writers, who also happen to be Mississippians, and he had the makings of a book.

I cannot resist the temptation to say here, who would have thought it? Because John Jones, if job applications mean anything at all, was on paper an unlikely prospect to deliver the candid, warm and insightful conversations with Mississippi's literary pantheon which he has produced. Of course things are not always what they seem, and I think that John was possibly the best prepared man in America to do this particular job.

Which was not immediately apparent. I hadn't kept up with John since he was a neighborhood boy to whom I gave a puppy of uncertain paternity. Since that time John had been through Boy Scouts, sports, college, and seeing the country. His last job before coming with us was picking and canning peas in a Jolly Green Giant factory in Washington state. Friendly and likeable, John was twenty-four years old and looked younger, ran everywhere instead of walking, and was never where he might be expected to be when he was expected to be there. All of this did not suggest a historian, oral or otherwise.

John's successful interviews clearly establish him as a competent oral historian. Eudora Welty called his questions "thoughtful and serious and sympathetic." I believe that he did his job so well because he was, and is, and ever shall be, a great reader. And what John did was to set forth on a straight and narrow path of his own choosing—an oral history of contemporary Mississippi literature. I believe that John's lifelong love of books and his broad knowledge of literature was the best possible preparation for the project which he undertook. And I think that his obvious familiarity with the works of the Mississippians he interviewed is what struck "the chord that vibrates" with them. He was able to establish an easy rapport with his subjects; the trust he inspired in them is evidenced by their frank and revealing replies to his searching and thoughtful questions. I am sure that these interviews contain information, opinions, and recollections never before recorded.

The Department of Archives and History is proud to present this first of two volumes, which we feel are an important contribution to Mississippi's cultural history. A valuable resource for students of American literature, this collection has the additional merit of being as delightful to read as some of the works of fiction discussed therein.

Charlotte Capers
Director of Publications
Department of Archives and History

Introduction

This is the first of two volumes containing interviews with eleven Mississippi writers. The interviews were collected as part of the oral history program of the Mississippi Department of Archives and History and were produced between 1979 and 1981. Included in this volume are interviews with Eudora Welty, Shelby Foote, Elizabeth Spencer, Barry Hannah, and Beth Henley. A second volume will include interviews with Walker Percy, Ellen Douglas, James Whitehead, Margaret Walker Alexander, Willie Morris, and Turner Cassity.

I am not sure that this book of interviews has anything to do with the method of historical investigation known as oral history. Although I approached the writers as an oral historian from the Mississippi Department of Archives and History, and each of the interviews was conducted with the understanding that it would become part of the permanent oral history collection of the Department, the project as a whole is not an orthodox oral history project. I believe that the best work an oral historian can do is to gather a record among scattered cultures which have no way beyond the spoken word to pass along to future generations the elements of their heritage. This premise would have precluded writers, who transmute experience into words that achieve some degree of permanence through publication. I chose writers as interviewee candidates because my interests and training were in literature, and the Department had a good collection of material on Mississippi writers which would be considerably enhanced by oral history interviews.

The interviews with Shelby Foote and Walker Percy form the core of this collection of conversations with Mississippi writers. Both were conducted before I decided to concentrate on the writers. Foote and Percy were interviewed in connection with an oral history of the Percy family of Greenville, Mississippi, in which I examined the cultural phenomenon in that area by focusing on the influence of William Alexander Percy, poet, planter, lawyer, teacher, adoptive father of Walker Percy and his brothers LeRoy and Phinizy, and author of *Lanterns on the Levee*. Much of the talk in both interviews centers on Will Percy and the larger question of how the complex and curious atmosphere in this state yielded writers of such quality over the past fifty years. I by no means limited our discussions to backgrounds and early influences, and in each case the interviewee moved easily into a more specific consideration of his work. I spent two afternoons with Shelby Foote at his home in Memphis in August 1979. Later I spent six hours with Walker Percy in a restaurant on the shores of Lake Pontchartrain and at his home in Covington, Louisiana. By the summer of 1980, with seven hours of taped conversation with two of the South's most respected writers, the project was under way.

The focus of the project was never rigidly defined. No underlying theme such as "place in fiction" or "the creative process" was pursued over the course of the interviewing. I never saw it as my function to constrict the thoughts of the writer by asking him to comment on my list of unifying elements in Southern fiction. I did bring some of the same questions before two or more writers, but those dealt mostly with their early backgrounds in the attempt to connect them with a time and place in Mississippi, if they had not already done so in their work. My aim was to avoid a dry and clichéd question and answer session, which would have denied the writers both space and provocation to discuss the growth of their art.

There are threads which unite the collection as a whole. In many cases my interests, and my naiveté, reappear to direct the flow of the conversation. Most of the writers discuss William Faulkner. I thought it would be valuable to have the Mississippi authors, who have had to deal with the weight of his achievement in fiction all their writing lives, analyze the relationship of their work to his. Another matter of concern is Mississippi itself. All of the interviewees had witnessed the social changes that occurred in the state during the 1960s, and it seemed useful to ask some of them to comment on the effect of an integrated society on the character of the people. I took Shelby Foote's charge that the college campus is no place for a serious, working writer, that the best writers earn their sustenance with the pen regardless of the sacrifice, to each of the interviewees who have had experience in academia. I also attempted to get the writers to hint at the source of their wonderful capacity to reach the reader by the correct ordering of the words people use every day. If there was anything more to the matter of craft than the reply, "I don't know. It's just what I do," I wanted it on tape.

But my basic intention was to elicit from each writer a lengthy discussion of his or her work. I wanted the writer to relate the genesis of a book, and then talk about the thematic center around which both the story and the characters gravitate. I tried to identify an overriding concern in the writer's mind which runs through the body of his work, and gives him the ambition, the energy and the infinite patience to create literature. These were large orders, and I think in some places I may have missed the signals altogether. But I had a unique opportunity to meet and talk with some of Mississippi's best minds, and it seemed the big questions were worth asking. All of the writers brought to the interviews considerable patience and good humor. Most of them had been interviewed many times before, but they took my questions with seriousness and answered them with candor.

We employed standard oral history methodology in preparing the interview transcripts. Each of the interviewees was given, and took, the opportunity to edit the first-draft, verbatim copy of his interview. The edited transcript was returned to me. I did some final editing before a perfect copy was typed and placed on file in the Department of Archives and History. Barry Hannah changed "spit" to "spat," and his interview, along with Welty's, Spencer's and Henley's, appears here in the same form in which it exists at the Archives. I did make some cuts in the seventy-two-page interview with Shelby Foote, but only in places where our talk evolved to the price of a loaf of bread. Because we chose to print the interviews in their entirety, some rambling occurs. My thought was that the rambling had a point, if only to show the mood of the interviewee on the day of our meeting. For these and other shortcomings in the interviews I take full responsibility and only hope that the reader finds some interest in what we discussed and the way we discussed it, and perhaps some patience of his own.

I wish to thank the staff at the Mississippi Department of Archives and History, most especially Patti Black, for their support and interest, and the good times. I was given freedom to work independently. I never took it for granted.

I would also like to thank the writers themselves, for receiving me with warmth and the kind of hospitality that showed me books are no greater than women or men.

John G. Jones

Mississippi Writers Talking

Photograph by Robert Williams

Eudora Welty

❧

May 13, 1981

We met at her home on a warm afternoon in mid-May. She still air-conditions only a few rooms in her house, so we kept an oscillating fan running at our feet as we talked. Scattered about the table surfaces in her living room was a variety of new books by some of her favorite female writers: *The Stories of Elizabeth Spencer, The Collected Stories of Elizabeth Bowen,* the former with a foreword by Miss Welty, an older copy of Virginia Woolf's *To the Lighthouse,* and, stacked in the corner of a work table behind me, a few copies of *The Collected Stories of Eudora Welty.* It seemed the right company for her. I hope the interview shows that at times she grew excited over the things we were discussing, assaulting the subject with wide-eyed interest, all the while swearing she didn't make any sense when she talked.

Welty: I once did a whole interview in New York for *The Paris Review.*
Jones: Sure. I read that.
Welty: Well, yes, but what happened was that none of it took. When the lady got home there was nothing.

Jones: I've done that.

Welty: And we had to do it again. That was awful, because she asked me the same questions and nothing was fresh anymore. I can answer spontaneously a lot better than I can if I think ahead. She asked me the same things.

Jones: Oh, no. You must have been good the first time.

Welty: Oh, it just wasn't very good.

Jones: It was.

Welty: A lot of it had to be written, you know. That's the hardest part about doing an interview because it turns out you have to write it too. I do. Now, this, though, is for oral records. It's done for . . .

Jones: For the state. I needed to explain this to you: As you did with Charlotte in the early '70s, you will see a copy of the transcript of our talk before we put it in the collection.

Welty: That's what's going to be hard. I swear I don't make any sense.

Jones: You do.

Welty: Charlotte and I, neither one of us made any sense on that one.

Jones: I like them. I read through all of them.

Welty: They really were silly.

Jones: No, they were fun to read because you all get along, and your conversation shows that.

Welty: Oh, yes. We thought it was a lot of fun.

Jones: Yes, ma'am. Let me say a few things. This is John Jones with the Mississippi Department of Archives and History. I'm on 1119 Pinehurst Street in Jackson, Mississipi, about to interview Miss Eudora Welty. This is my first time to interview Miss Welty, it's about the fifth or sixth tape you've done with the Department of Archives and History, and it's about the 170th time you've been interviewed. I didn't want to repeat any of the information that Charlotte was able to get from you. I just wanted to ask you some general questions about your career, your writing, your art.

Welty: Anything you want to. I haven't got a very good memory about dates, but that's all right.

Jones: Fine.

Welty: We can check up on that later.

Jones: Yes, because you will be getting a transcript of this later.

Welty: Oh, yes.

Jones: Let me ask you this first: In talking with these Mississippi writers as I've done it's interesting to find out when they first got the impulse to sit down and write; when the creative impulse first took control of their lives. Do you remember when that happened to you?

Welty: No, I don't. I couldn't put my finger on it. I think in my case I almost couldn't notice the transition between loving to read and loving to write, because I've always been a reader. I love stories. Actually I can't remember when I felt, "Now I'm going to write something." It seemed to be sort of a natural overflow. Maybe I always wanted to write. How do I know? But I had no revelation that that was what I wanted to do. I'm glad, because I would have been rather startled if I had taken it too—if I had felt a responsibility or something of "being a writer." I'm glad it didn't happen too soon. It would have stopped me.

Jones: Yes, that's a point I've heard made before. It seems like it would be intensely intimidating for a young person who, after reading the best of American literature, might think that that's what they wanted to do with their life.

Welty: Yes.

Jones: So it's really a gradual process?

Welty: I think so. What always remained with me was the love of the story, whether I was reading or writing it. I didn't have any self-consciousness about the writ-

ing, which I think I would have had if I'd felt a stern command to go and write. I don't know that anyone does have that. It was so natural for me to want to do it. In fact, at one point Katherine Anne Porter, who was always kind and helpful to me from the beginning when my stories first appeared in *Southern Review*, had invited me to Yaddo, a colony up in New York State near Saratoga, where artists of various kinds had studios to themselves and were given privacy and time to work and so on. It was just everything you dream of as a writer. But at that time I didn't dream of it because I seemed to write in connection with everything else I did too. When I was put into this silent studio with a sign on the door saying "Silence. Writer at Work," I was so self-conscious I could not write anything. I think that's the way I would've felt if I felt I'd had a calling to do it. It was much better to just take it as part of life. I never have felt a divorce between my life and work, except the act itself, of course, which is something done in solitude and with much thinking. But I never have felt cut off by my work. I never have felt isolated and the things people always say, you know, like, "Isn't it a very lonely life?" I think I must have been very blessed that I didn't have a feeling of self-consciousness, of being picked out to be a writer.
Jones: So what did make you sit down to write that first story?
Welty: "Death of a Traveling Salesman"?
Jones: Yes, ma'am.
Welty: I know why I wrote that story. This was in the Depression. A friend of our family traveled for the Mississippi Highway Department. He went into the remote parts of Mississippi, and bought up property for the right-of-way for them. He went into the most far-flung places. When he came back one day he said he'd been up there somewhere, and he told a tale. It had nothing to do with "Death of a Traveling Salesman,"

but he quoted this man saying they didn't have any fire
and he had to go to Mr. Somebody's house and "borry
some fire." Well, those words just hit me. They were
electrical. You could just see a whole situation from
that. It was just so far back in time, and so remote. It
made me think of something very far away and elementary about life; elemental, whichever it is. So I wrote
that story then, you know, just from hearing that remark. I was working toward "I had to go borry some
fire," and the story sort of grew from that. I think all
my stories have grown from something in life and not
from other sources like a book, no literary sources.
They never remain in a story as themselves. They are
transformed and made into something else, but they
come out of real life.

Jones: Yes. And from "Death of a Traveling Salesman"
through *The Optimist's Daughter* certainly your place has
not changed, but your theme is something it seems to
me you've been developing from the start.

Welty: I'm glad you think so. I think I must have. I'm
sure I have.

Jones: I wanted to ask if early you saw a void that you
could fill through your writing from the very first.

Welty: I don't quite know what you mean by "a void."

Jones: That there was a void in Mississippi literature
even, and . . .

Welty: Oh, no. I don't think about anything else,
other people, me, when I am writing; just the story. I
don't have those feelings of ambition, either. There's no
time to because you're thinking about the work. Of
course I love to do things well, and when I feel like I've
done something as well as I can I am pleased about it.
But at the time I'm working I don't know whether it's
good or bad. I just want to do the best I can for that
story. Each story is like a new challenge or a new
adventure, and I don't find help anywhere, or look for
it anywhere, except inside.

Jones: So there was never a long-range plan to develop these stories toward something, some theme?

Welty: Oh, no. I think that would've paralyzed me too. No, the thing at hand is the one. I see now how that refers to that question you asked me, but I didn't have an overall idea about working toward something. I think such things evolve of themselves out of the work. It sort of teaches you as you go. You learn what you're writing about, in one sense, through the work. Of course you know what you want to do, your destination and your direction in a story, but you also learn a whole lot of things about that destination and direction through the work. That's why you like it.

Jones: I know you have said that your W. P. A. experience planted in you the germ that grew into your becoming a writer. I know your father was from Ohio and was president of Lamar Life Insurance Company. Your mother was from West Virginia. Your father being a banker/businessman, what did he think of the New Deal and Franklin Roosevelt, and your work with the W. P. A.?

Welty: Oh, poor man, he died before then. He died in 1931, shortly after the bank failures and everything.

Jones: Oh, that's right.

Welty: So he never knew any of that. He was not always a businessman. He was born on a farm in Ohio. He was a country school teacher. He lived in the country and came from country people. When he decided to marry my mother, another schoolteacher, they decided to make a new life for themselves in a different part of the world, and they selected Jackson. He came down here and got a job with what later turned out to be the Lamar Life. It was, you know, a lowly job—bookkeeper, I think. Would he have been about your age? I think so. He just worked his way up. He always stayed with that company. He loved it. He was a businessman. But he was for me being a writer, but he

8

said, wisely, that I needed to be able to support myself some other way, because you can hardly sell stories and earn a living that way. I'd never thought about that one way or the other. It was, of course, true. So that's what I did.

Jones: Good advice.

Welty: It was good advice. But he never knew that I became a writer and I don't know what he would've thought about what I did.

Jones: I know in reading the criticism of your work much ado is made of the fact that your mother and father weren't from the Deep South, but I've never heard you comment on it. I was wondering if the fact that they were from the North and upper South made your perceptions of southern life that much more acute.

Welty: It could have been, but you see, although my mother came from West Virginia, was born there, she was from Virginia stock on both sides. She considered herself a Southerner of the first water. I think something to do with the Civil War and anti-slavery was why they moved to West Virginia. They set their slaves free—at least on one side; I don't know about the other—and went to West Virginia where there was no slavery. They were Methodist preachers, the men; one was a Baptist preacher. They went over there out of a sense of bringing up their family in West Virginia. My mother was a Southerner and a Democrat. My father was a Yankee and a Republican. They were very different in everything. At that time there weren't very many Republicans in Mississippi. I was very worried about that. I think there were maybe two in Jackson that I knew of.

Jones: Hiding.

Welty: I don't know. So my parents used to have good political discussions at the table all the time. It was interesting to grow up learning there were two sides to everything. It made you think.

Jones: That's interesting. So your mother was indeed a Southerner, and you had that kind of heritage too.

Welty: Yes.

Jones: "Death of a Traveling Salesman" came out in 1936.

Welty: Yes.

Jones: Even then in Mississippi there was an established literary tradition. I was wondering if that meant anything to you when you began writing? Had you at that time read Mr. Faulkner and other Mississippi writers?

Welty: I hadn't read Faulkner then for the reason that you almost couldn't find books of his. I tried to. They weren't in the library. You know, he was almost out of print until Malcolm Cowley brought out the *Portable*. I used to buy his books second hand in New Orleans and places, and I read them as I could find them. But I didn't connect myself to any kind of tradition or to any other writer. It never occurred to me that my work—I didn't know what it would be—would be taken seriously enough to "place." I was just reading his books because I loved to read them, and not that I could emulate—indeed I never did emulate. Of course as time went on, Faulkner became much more accessible and much more widely appreciated in his home state, which took some doing.

Jones: Which occurred after Stockholm, in the '50s?

Welty: Yes, but he got back in print before that. That's when Fred Sullens on the *Jackson Daily News* used to lash out at him. I believe he once included me in the "Garbage Can School of Literature." I don't recall why. He could never have read anything. But he thought we all could be lumped together. He put a whole bunch in there. Faulkner had that to contend with. He got to be well known, but not accepted by any means.

Jones: Did you meet and talk with him ever? Do you remember your first meeting with him?

Welty: Yes, I surely do. I went to Oxford with a
friend who'd gone to Ole Miss, and I stayed with an old
friend of his, Miss Ella Somerville. You probably know
who she is.

Jones: Yes. Charlotte and I have talked about her.

Welty: Yes. She was a marvelous lady, and a contemporary and friend of Faulkner's. She gave a small dinner
party, and they were invited along with Bob Farley and
all these other friends of Faulkner's. So I met him under
those wonderful auspices of Miss Ella's home at her
table when the conversation was among all old friends
and I was the new person. So that was the most natural
way to meet anyone. I never got to know him well.

Jones: What year was that first meeting?

Welty: I don't know. I believe it was in the '40s. But
William Faulkner and I never had a conversation about
writing, of course. He did invite me to come out to the
house, and I did. We had a nice time, told tales. He
never brought up writing, and you know I wouldn't
have done it. But we never had any kind of literary—no
ties between us at all. But one time, William Faulkner,
when he was in Hollywood, wrote me a letter, and I
misplaced it, couldn't find it high or low. I looked for
it over many years. Well, I've just found out what
happened to it. I had sent it—bragging!—to a friend in
Oxford to read—one of the group who knew William
Faulkner—not Miss Ella. There it remained forgotten
among her letters until last year when one of her relations found it, the letter from Faulkner, and put it with
the letter that it was enclosed in, and sold it to the
University of Virginia for what they say was a horrendous sum. I heard about it from the University of Virginia. They wrote and said, "You'll be interested to
know that we have this letter." I wrote back and said,
"So that's where it is! Doesn't it belong to me?" They
said, "Unfortunately, it belongs to the Commonwealth
of Virginia." I thought that was awful, and I wrote her
an indignant letter. It wasn't her fault, but I just didn't

think that should be true. I said, "Would you at least send me a Xerox copy so I can read it again?" She did. But don't you think that's funny?

Jones: Yes, I sure do.

Welty: See, I'd just published my little book *The Robber Bridegroom*, and he said he thought it was good, and "Is there anything I can do for you in Hollywood?" Wasn't that wonderful?

Jones: Yes.

Welty: And I couldn't find it! That was the nearest we ever came to talking about anybody's work, his or mine.

Jones: What do you think he meant by "Is there anything I can do for you?"

Welty: I think in Hollywood, probably. Wouldn't you? He said "I will be here until . . . " whatever it was.

Jones: Yes. We'll leave Mr. Faulkner for a minute. The other great literary strain in Mississippi at that time came from the Percy family in Greenville. I don't know if you were aware of this, but I've done a number of interviews with people who knew Will Percy.

Welty: Oh, how wonderful. I'd love to hear them.

Jones: It's a fascinating family.

Welty: Absolutely! I agree with you, from the ones I know now.

Jones: Yes, ma'am. And I know you said in your address at the inaugural ceremonies for the governor that at one time in your memory Greenville was a town of 20,000 people, and had seventeen published authors.

Welty: Those figures may not be exactly accurate.

Jones: They're close. I was wondering if you ever got to know Will Percy.

Welty: No. In those days I don't think young people went anywhere and met someone the way they do now, the way that students do. I wish I could've met him, but I never did. I read him. In the mid '40s I did get

to know Hodding Carter, that is young Hodding's
father, and Ben Wasson, and all those people who did
know him, and Shelby Foote. All of them did know
Mr. Will Percy. David Cohn. He seemed a very real
presence to me, a bulwark up there. But it is a marvelous family. What a good thing you've done.

Jones: It's been fun.

Welty: I'm sure.

Jones: But there's something remarkable about the fact
that in that small place there could've been Walker
Percy, Shelby Foote, Ellen Douglas. . .

Welty: Yes, I met her too at the same time. That was
before she began to write, I think.

Jones: Yes. Early in your career, who influenced you
among the female writers across America? Were there
any great influences?

Welty: I don't know, John. I never can put my finger
on these things for sure. Of course I was influenced. I
love to read, and I adore what I read. You know that
it's worked on me, but not in any specific way I can
think of, not in any immediate ways when I work. I
can just do some detective work after the fact. I must
have learned this or that from this or that person, but
not consciously.

Jones: No big book that changed your life?

Welty: I suppose Chekhov would come closest to it,
and also Katherine Mansfield, and Virginia Woolf. Of
course, those people are not Americans. Willa Cather,
did, but I was kind of slow finding her. I wish I had
had the sense to read her sooner. One time I just sat
down and read it all through. That's what I love to do:
from start to finish. Let me think. Fairy tales and
myths in my childhood reading had a profound effect
on me. That was not always indirect; sometimes it was
direct. In those stories called *The Golden Apples* I just
made free with them—and *The Robber Bridegroom*. And
the Bible, because I love to read the Old Testament.

The Old Testament has the best stories. The King
James Version stays with you forever, rings and rings in
your ears. Oh, *Don Quixote*. That feeling of discovery
you get with such a novel is the most marvelous thing.
A door has been opened. I've just now been trying to
write about Virginia Woolf's novel *To the Lighthouse*.
Harcourt Brace is getting out a new edition of three of
her novels, and they're having a living woman writer to
write a little foreword for each; just sort of what it
means to you. So I'm doing the one that meant the
most to me which was *To the Lighthouse*. I've been trying to describe that feeling you get when you come
upon something. I came upon it absolutely cold and it
just knocked me out. I've read it lots of times since,
but I read it again in order to write this piece, and it
did the same thing. So I know, even though I couldn't
show in my work, heavens, the sense of what she has
done certainly influenced me as an artist. Mark Twain
and Ring Lardner I loved. I read them when I was
growing up.

Jones: That's a good list.

Welty: I suppose it must show how varied a writer's
loves can be, and what a great circumference the reading covers.

Jones: Yes.

Welty: I've had people say to me, "Do you ever read
anyone else's work?" That has always just amazed me.
People would ask me down at the library, "What are
you doing at the library? Are you interested in other
peoples' work?" I just think that's amazing!

Jones: When you published *A Curtain of Green* in 1941
the critics, reviewers, said, "Here's the spontaneous
work of a born writer." Two questions about that: Is
writing for you spontaneous? And, of course, is there
such a thing as a born writer?

Welty: Who knows about the born writer? I couldn't
answer that. It would be terrible if you were either a

born writer or not, and that it all depended on that. It would be kind of like, "Are you saved?"

Jones: Elected. Right.

Welty: I don't know about that, but as far as spontaneous goes I can answer that exactly. That first book of stories really was spontaneous. They were almost never revised. They would've been the better for it. It never occurred to me. I thought you sat down and wrote a story sort of the way you read—you know, you just sit down and write it. That was how they were left. They did have a certain quality of the spontaneous that, I suppose, I have lost over the years because I now know there are dozens of ways you can do everything, especially since the longer you write the more possibilities occur to you. As long as you are writing a story, its possibilities are endless. So, I don't know. I think they have gained, I hope they have gained something by being carefully revised. I do a lot of editing. They might have lost some of the spontaneity. I still write the first draft spontaneously. I hope I have enough sense, I don't always, to keep the true thing in there; the one that hits it on the head; that's really it. I hope I have enough sense to know it and not tamper with it. It may not be perfect, but it has got something that shouldn't be altered.

Jones: Following *A Curtain of Green* came *The Robber Bridegroom* the very next year, then *The Wide Net,* and then *Delta Wedding* in, I believe, '46.

Welty: I think so. I wrote it during World War II, so it must have come out soon after that.

Jones: That was my question. That was a period of incredible output for you, during the war.

Welty: That's not exactly as it seems, because it took me so long to get published. When I got out *A Curtain of Green* I already had most of the stories in *The Wide Net* on the way, anyway. I'd been trying for quite a long time to get them published. So, although they all came out just about the same time, I'd been sending them around for years. I caught up with myself with *The Wide Net.* I think I could have published *The Wide Net* almost at once after *A Curtain of Green,* but the publishers were hoping I'd write something long in between. *The Robber Bridegroom* is really just a little tale. It was the publication that made it seem like a short novel, not the writer. I did write fast and quite a lot.

Jones: It's such an achievement! Do you remember when your period of greatest productivity was? Was it following *A Curtain of Green,* during the war?

Welty: I don't know. That's when I was doing *Delta Wedding.* Also, most of these times I had a job too and I was working on nonfiction bits and pieces and things like that. I think the time when I went through the most intense, sustained writing was when I did the collection called *The Golden Apples.* These stories were revealing themselves as interrelated. I wasn't sure quite in what way. That came a little later to me. Halfway through I realized the big connection there, the deep connections. But I was writing without stop, going from one story to the other, a sustained burst. It was writing something as long as a novel but as stories. Also I was very happy writing that book. I loved working on those stories. I love that period.

Jones: Yes. That's my personal favorite.

Welty: Is it really?

Jones: Yes, *The Golden Apples.*

Welty: Oh, I'm glad.

Jones: Yes, ma'am. It may be the best thing I've ever read. Honestly.

Welty: I'm terribly glad you like that. I don't find many people are familiar with it.

Jones: There's not a better story than "June Recital" anywhere.

Welty: Oh, thank you.

Jones: We'll talk about *The Golden Apples* some more

in a minute. Also during the Second World War you were writing first as Eudora Welty and then, under the pseudonym Michael Ravenna, reviews of front line World War II action . . .

Welty: I wrote some reviews and signed them that, but they weren't front line war things. That was a mischievous figment of imagination on the part of Nash Burger of Jackson, Mississippi. I think they were mostly about art the soldiers drew in the war and things like that. It was because I was working on the *New York Times Book Review* at that time, and they didn't like the staff to sign reviews because we were supposed to get other people to do the reviews. When we couldn't we would do them and sign them.

Jones: I don't think that detracts from my point, which is—I hope you don't take any offense at this . . .

Welty: No, of course not.

Jones: But here you were, a lady from Jackson, Mississippi; obviously there wasn't a whole lot about war that you knew about firsthand. And in your early stories, in a story like "Powerhouse," how a woman from Jackson, Mississippi, a white woman, could have known and put down on paper the life and words of a musician, and a black musician at that, like Powerhouse, is an amazing achievement in anyone's eyes. Can you tell me something, maybe by illustrating the story "Powerhouse," that could hint at the answer?

Welty: Well, I can tell you as well as anyone could about "Powerhouse." I know exactly how that came about. I loved the music of Fats Waller and had all his records. He played here in Jackson at a program sort of like the one, well, just like the one I described. I went and watched him, and I was just captivated by his presence, in addition to the music, which I already knew and was familiar with. As you know, I'm not a musician like your father [Howard Jones].

Jones: But you knew the lingo, and the lingo of a black musician.

Welty: Oh, I was listening to them. I was one of those people who were just hanging around listening. Of course, what I was trying to do was to express something about the music in the story. I wanted to express what I thought of as improvisation, which I was watching them do, by making him improvise this crazy story, which I just made up as I went. Nothing like that, of course, happened. I didn't hear anything like that. But I made it up to illustrate the feeling I got a sense of among the musicians; how they talked to each other. There was this sort of inner core of musicians, and this outer core. I have no idea what they did at intermission. Everything I wrote is made up except the program itself and the impression it made on me, both hearing and seeing it. I had no idea I was going to write anything when I went to that. I would've thought, rightly, "You don't know anything." It's true, I didn't. But I was so excited by the evening that I wrote it, after I got home. And the next day when I woke up I said, "How could I have had the nerve to do something like that?" But I did have the sense to know that there was no use in me trying to correct or revise or anything. It was that or nothing, because it had to be written at that moment, or not at all. I could not have gone back over it and tried to shape it or do something constructive like that. You know, I just left it. But that was a one time thing. I couldn't write another story like "Powerhouse." I don't see how I wrote that one. It was just the music, that's what did it. But that's valid!

Jones: Yes'm.

Welty: I don't see why not.

Jones: Also, as people all over the world have pointed out, you knew and got down the language of everyone who speaks through your stories. In that vein I was

wondering if you could tell me to what extent your
experience was translated in the stories and to what
extent your fiction is written to make up for what your
experience lacks, what is missing in your experience? I
guess another way to ask it, and this is maybe high-
falutin, but does life give literature meaning for the
artist, or does literature give your life meaning? You
understand what I'm asking?

Welty: Up until the last I thought I did. Does life
give literature meaning or does literature give life
meaning. Is there a choice? It's such an intimate relationship. I don't really separate them. The life blood of
one is in the other. I don't know. Your question began
with the way people talk. It's one of the things that has
always absorbed me because I love to listen to people
talk. Cut that off and let me get some water.

Jones: I've choked you. I'm sorry.

Welty: No. I'll be back.

Jones: Yes, ma'am.

(Break)

Jones: Let me reiterate that question.

Welty: Okay.

Jones: I was asking to what extent does your fiction
come out of your life's experiences, and to what extent
is your fiction written to sort of make up for the missed
experiences in life?

Welty: I can answer that. You can't write about any
feeling or emotion that you've not experienced. But I
don't like to write autobiographically. What I like to
do is invent the characters, situation, action that
dramatizes it, which will act out my emotions. I know
how these invented people feel, or I couldn't write it;
but I give them other, comparable reasons to feel that
way. I don't think you could even begin to make up
grief, or love, or something. I'm always alert to anything going on in life that gives me a clue or gives me a
starting point on a dramatic situation, that would let

this emotion unfold in a way that I can handle it on paper. When some clue comes along you realize it. Maybe it's a news item in the paper or an overheard remark, or the experience of someone that you know about. And then all of this accumulation of your own experience of feeling finds a way to be communicated in a better way than your own life does it, more dramatically, anyway. So to simplify it, that's what my own writing process is. There's no way of knowing what others' is. So I often write about some things it would seem to you I wouldn't know about, but I know about them deeply in my own experience, of my own perceiving, or I would not want to write about them. Well, I've never murdered anybody. I have murders in my stories. But I can certainly feel and understand anger. And so on.

Jones: That's a wonderful answer.

Welty: To show you my reservations about not writing about what I don't know: I wrote one book of stories all laid in Europe, but I had to write every one of them from the point of view of the traveler or the outsider.

Jones: *The Bride of Innisfallen.*

Welty: I don't know how Italians or Irish—I don't know enough. All I know is the overheard, the observed. I don't know firsthand. The point of entry is what you're looking for, then you can go ahead. All the rest is simply general human nature in which we all share.

Jones: I believe you call it the point in which people reveal themselves.

Welty: Well, in this sense I just mean the point you can get in. When I wrote that novel *Delta Wedding*—I don't know much about the Delta, which I probably don't need to tell you. So I made my person a little girl nine years old.

Jones: Sure. Laura.

Welty: She knew just about what I knew. In that way I could venture as far as I liked. I could tell my story, but I wasn't telling it as an old hand at the Delta. I didn't know it, except how to get there from here.

Jones: In this sense, let me ask you something about your use of humor. Walker Percy said that there is something in the modern consciousness so that there is communication from writer to reader which is greatly facilitated by humor.

Welty: Yes. That's interesting.

Jones: In your work, especially as seen in "The Petrified Man," "Why I Live at the P. O." and *The Ponder Heart,* humor is used extensively. Even though you have ridiculous events and characters in many ways, you never tell it ridiculously. I was wondering if you could talk about your use of humor, its function in your work.

Welty: I don't know. I think it's one of the hardest subjects in the world to speak about. Don't you? In a way it may be a way of entry, too, through humor. It's a way to try, risk something, a way to get around something to make it endurable, to live with it or to shrug it off. And then it's inherent in a whole lot of living, I think. I think it's just there. It's there! If you can show it and make it a process of revealing, that would be its justification; not for its own sake but to show something. People show an awful lot of things through humor, both conscious and unconscious. Don't you think so?

Jones: Yes, ma'am.

Welty: I think it also can take form as something Southern. We've always appreciated humor and humorous things. We've also contributed to the humorous.

Jones: Certainly you have. Is it a different frame of mind that you're in when you sit down to write something like "Why I Live at the P. O.?"

Welty: Those are early stories. I don't know why I wrote them except to show how people talked. I love to write dialogue but it's very hard to prune it and make it sharp and make it advance the plot and reveal the characters—both characters—the one listening and the one talking. You can use it to do all kinds of things. I like to do it because it's hard, I guess. I really like it. I laugh when I write those things.

Jones: I loved *The Ponder Heart,* and I was interested to see that Miss Capers played Edna Earle in the production . . .

Welty: At the Little Theatre, yes.

Jones: I asked her about it, but she didn't feel like talking about it very much.

Welty: She was very funny; she was Charlotte, of course, and it worked out really well. It was the earliest production I had seen, except for the original one on Broadway.

Jones: *The Golden Apples* came out in 1949. I read it for the first time in preparation for this interview and found it to be my favorite of what you've written. It was so good and complete I couldn't think of a good question to ask you about it other than to just ask you to comment on it a bit more, and maybe tell me something about the idea behind it and what interested you about the golden apples myth?

Welty: Well, you know, now I think I'd think twice before I threw around myths and everything so freely. I'm glad I did then because I just used them as freely as I would the salt and pepper. They were part of my life, like poetry, and I would take something from Yeats here and something from a myth there. I had no *system* about it. But people write papers on these things and they just make things up. I got one in the mail last night.

Jones: A dissertation?

Welty: It's the beginning of one. Somebody out in

California has written it. You don't want to hear about
that. What those people do is not treat your work as
fiction; in fact they don't seem to know the difference
between fiction and anthropology and mythology. . .
Jones: Sociology.
Welty: They are making your work fit in with their
scheme—*their* myth. "Well, if Virgie was. . ." I forget
who Virgie was supposed to be, ". . . and the boy Loch
is really Perseus, then Easter is, or should have been,
the Medusa." Well, equivalents like that are all apart
from my intention. I used them in the way I think life
does. Life recalls them. These likenesses occur to you
when you are living your life. They are plucked out of
here and there because they seem to apply. I wanted to
show mainly in that collection something about illusion
in our lives—I made a little town where everybody was
living in a sort of dream world, and I called it Morgana.
Jones: Sure.
Welty: The name is sort of like the Fata Morgana, or
sea mirage, but it worked in with the Delta, where
people often named a town after a family and just added
an a: Morgan-a. It seemed right. Everybody was sort of
trapped in their own dream world there, or were ap-
prehensive of leaving,of getting outside of it; all but
Virgie who really was and is a courageous and fine
person.
Jones: Talented.
Welty: I love Virgie.
Jones: I do too.
Welty: I did not realize until I'd written half of these
stories that all these people really did live in Morgana.
So I was just showing different phases of it, different
aspects. They were all under the same compulsion. I
realized that the stories were connected. It was a marvelous moment with me when I realized that a story I'd
written really was about a character from an earlier

story. My subconscious mind, I guess, had been working on the same lines all the time. Everything slid into place like a jigsaw puzzle. It all worked out. I loved it because I felt that I could get deeper into all the people through using a number of stories and different times in their lives than I could hope to do using one story.

Jones: Did "Music from Spain" come in the same creative burst?

Welty: Yes. It came in last. I wanted to show somebody from Morgana who'd gone outside the local circle; and yet he was no better outside than he would've been inside. It was such a strange story. I wrote it, as you can tell, in San Francisco. It's kind of a love letter to San Francisco on the side. But I never knew for certain if I should include that with the other stories or not. What did you think? Did you feel it was dragged in?

Jones: No'm, I didn't. I wanted to find out what happened to the other brother of Miss Snowdie's two twins.

Welty: Well, I think I had been wondering too as I went along, and then when I was in San Francisco I thought, "Here he is."

Jones: "I found him!"

Welty: Yes.

Jones: I knew that it had been in the Levee Press edition.

Welty: They printed it before *The Golden Apples* came out. It was already part of the book.

Jones: You did not write it expressly for the Levee Press?

Welty: No. It was just something I had that had not been printed.

Jones: Right. What about Virgie Rainey? Your eyes seemed to light up when you talked about her. Is she one of your favorites? Is she somewhat closer to your own condition?

Welty: No, I don't think so. I suppose vaguely we would connect somewhere, like the feeling of indepen-

dence, and of wanting to do something about your life
for yourself. But I gave her a musical talent about
which I know nothing. Certainly I had a music teacher
who rapped me with a fly swatter, but I didn't know
too much about music. I heard it all the time because
Belhaven at that time had open windows, and all those
pieces in there came straight across the street from
Belhaven. I just put them in my story. I wanted to give
her the outlet of some art. I felt that need about myself,
and I felt that independence. But that's such
generalities. I guess I felt a part of everybody in the
book, every one of them. You have to if you're going to
be a writer.

Jones: The Big Black River.

Welty: Yes, the Big Black, Vicksburg.

Jones: What about the dangers at that time of creating
another mythical county in Mississippi? Were you in-
timidated by the county to the north?

Welty: Oh, no, because mine's just on no scale. It was
just something that served. Faulkner created an entire
world; all the history of Mississippi and the Indians and
everything. Mine was just an appropriate location I
wanted to mean something for that set of stories.

Jones: You weren't scared of the inevitable comparison?

Welty: It never occurred to me. There isn't any comparison. You know. Every writer has to create his stage,
the set. The setting is fundamental to a story.

Jones: Yes. Let me ask you something that may be a
little too general but I think is to the point in terms of
your work. From Virgie to Laurel McKelva, there
seems to be something you are saying about the importance and significance of memory, of holding on to
memory. Walker Percy calls it living in some authentic
relation to the chief events of one's life. This seems so
important for the characters in your work.

Welty: Yes.

Jones: I was reading an interesting review of a children's book by a man named Maurice Sendak.

Welty: Oh, yes, I've got it. I've got that book!

Jones: I haven't read the book, or seen it.

Welty: I'll show it to you.

Jones: In the review Sendak is quoted as saying that writing this book has made him a happy man, has put him in touch with a memory that he had but wasn't aware of, which released for him all kinds of possibilities.

Welty: Yes, yes.

Jones: Do you think that there is in a person's memory something that can make him happy?

Welty: Oh, yes. I certainly do. To me memory is terribly important, a source and a force, too. If you've ever tried to go back and recall *all* of something—you may not be old enough yet—but you do realize that there're things back there you had no idea were still there. The more you try to remember, the more comes up. It's like Thomas Mann said in *Joseph and His Brethren,* the past is a well. It's wonderful to think of, that it's all there, all your experience, down deep in your memory. Writing does the same thing, it brings your past to the surface. I don't often put really straight autobiographical things in my work, but when I wrote *The Optimist's Daughter,* all that part about West Virginia was true. That all came back to me when I started thinking about it. I had remembered it in general, but not as much as came back. The fact of learning what it is you remember is instructive. How do you store this up? Why? I think any writer has more to thank memory for than most anything. I don't mean writing about the past. What you remember can apply just as well to something you are writing today. You learned it through something in your memory, but you use it for anything that you might wish. You might be writing about the future. I hadn't realized—I know what you are thinking about

now: that last story in *The Golden Apples,* where Virgie
is remembering everything.

Jones: Yes.

Welty: I realized that myself when I was doing proof-
reading. I'd forgotten what I did at the end of that
book, you know, in precise detail. I remember what I
was trying to do, but not what I had done. I hadn't
connected that with Laurel McKelva, but there certainly is a connection.

Jones: Oh, yes.

Welty: I'm grateful to you for thinking of it. I never
do connect any book with any other book, and when
someone is able to point out a connection I'm fascinated. It's something else that your mind has done
that you're not aware of. One may have led to the
other. Virgie and Laurel were such different people,
backgrounds and everything, but they were doing the
same thing. I'm glad you told me that.

Jones: And Laurel finds the breadboard her dead husband made for her mother, and in releasing the breadboard, by letting it stay in the house with Fay, she is
making a commitment through memory to her future,
she is able to live on without being drowned by memory.

Welty: Yes, yes.

Jones: That's one of the most fascinating things in
your work to me.

Welty: Well, it fascinates me in itself, the process of
memory. Also, it seems to have its own timers, and it
comes to you at very strange times. You know, you can
wake up in the morning and it will present you with
something; the way it used to work your math problems. You wake up the next morning and it would be
worked. Your memory puts that together too, even
though it doesn't know any math.

Jones: And with characters like Wanda Fay McKelva,
and Bonnie Dee Peacock in *The Ponder Heart* people

who live without memory, is that their greatest afflic-
tion? I don't even know how to ask that.

Welty: I think you ask it well, and I agree. I think it
is one of their greatest afflictions. If they had memory it
would've taught them something about the present.
They have nothing to draw on. They don't understand
their own experience. And they would have to under-
tand it in order to have it in their memory. Their
memory hasn't received it because it hasn't meant anything. That is putting it in blatant words. It certainly
isn't simple like that.

Jones: Also one of the things you are indicting in your
work is noncommunication between people. I remember one of the interesting things you said about Tennessee Williams characters was that they never break
through the "sound barrier of communication." Is non-
communication the real enemy in human understanding, in our modern world?

Welty: I suppose so. That is at least the effect. I don't
know the cause of it. It might be different. The *effect*
might be non-communication. I was thinking about
the plays of Chekhov. You know, the characters sit
around, and none of them are really talking to one
another, they are just talking like this; yet they possibly love each other, they feel their private emotions.
They don't really talk to each other, and Chekhov uses
that dramatically to show the human predicament. It
does. It does show it.

Jones: Like the ladies talking in the back yard of the
McKelva house in *The Optimist's Daughter* denigrating
Fay, and Laurel won't listen to them and goes back in
the house.

Welty: Yes.

Jones: Yes. That's interesting. Creating as you have
this world of characters—I hope this isn't too personal
to ask you—this vast world of totally alive people, have
they taken the place of anything so that you don't need

as many personal connections in your own life?
Welty: No, no, they couldn't do that. They came from
me. I mean, my feelings of affection and admiration
and all that couldn't go to somebody I've made up.
Jones: Sure. I hadn't thought of it that way.
Welty: You know what I mean. No, they don't take
the place of real human beings. I love my characters,
but as characters. They don't live in this house. They're
real to me, but they're in my mind, not in the world. I
like people in the world.
Jones: Yes, ma'am. I don't have too many more questions. I appreciate your patience. I've also done an oral
history of the civil rights movement in Mississippi.
Welty: Oh, yes.
Jones: I've talked with a number of people, black and
white, involved in those times. You have an interesting
quote in your essay "Must the Novelist Crusade?"
which I thought answered most all questions I might
ask you in this area. But you do say, "Entering the
hearts and minds of our own people is no harder now
than it ever was, I suppose." You wrote this in '65.
"Entering the hearts and minds of our own people . . ."
which is, as you say, what the novelist is trying to do,
"is no harder now than it ever was, I suppose." I heard
William Styron speaking at a literary symposium at
Millsaps with Willie Morris and Governor Winter, and
he said people are no more fragmented now than
they've ever been. One thing I did want to ask you is
has this great turnabout that happened in Mississippi in
the 1960s, this new direction in terms of race relations
which occurred, has this changed the hearts and minds
of the people?
Welty: That's a thoughtful question. I think I was
mistaken in what you read about it being no harder
than it ever was. I was sincere as far as I knew, but I
didn't know enough. It was harder. I think more effort
had to be made, and that it was made, you know, as

time went on. We had to learn to do it. I was thinking of the people whose hearts were in the right place, but that wasn't enough. It took more learning. I think we've been through an experience which was more profound than we'd guessed; both black and white. Now we are both more open in a way that—well, I had not experienced it because it had never happened. Now, seeing how much more there was to communication than the wish, and the desire, and the heart, I feel I have more to learn now than I had to learn then.

Jones: Yes. In talking about the effect of the civil rights movement, here's an argument or a point I'm sure you've heard made 100 times: That one of the factors which contributed to the fact that there were so many writers from Mississippi was the treatment of the black man, that sense of guilt.

Welty: Yes.

Jones: Now that that's removed—certainly it is for my generation—is that going to have an effect on Mississippi being a spawning ground for writers?

Welty: Well, I think all writers have to reflect their own times, you know, whatever they are. Everything changes in time. No writer could write about today in the same way that he might have written back in the '50s, or the '60s, or in ways the '70s, because everything is different. I don't mean that he would change his sensibilities or his understanding. That remains the constant, his openness to what he's trying to write about. The subject itself would be very different. The problem is not the same now. The writer would be the same, I think. I don't know if he would have an identity as "a writer of Mississippi." I don't see why not. But whatever it is, he's got to write about life as he knows it, or else it won't be worth doing, and he won't be fulfilling his role, or obligation, as an artist. You've got to write about what you see. Whatever comes next, you've got to handle it. Do you agree?

Jones: Yes, ma'am. I do. I suppose the crux of the
question was is there something basic, deep-down, that
has changed in the Mississippi character that you see?

Welty: I feel at least for now, I don't know how long
it will last, that the Southerner, the Mississippian, has
got a character that does stem from his sense of place
and of the significance of history and so on. That hasn't
changed. I don't mean he's living in the past. I'm not
talking about that. It's just a sense of continuity that
has always characterized us, I think; a knowledge of
family stories, that sense of generations and continuity.
That gives us an identity. I think that's still there. I
don't think there would be any point in trying to eradi-
cate that.

Jones: I've saved a couple of hard ones for the end. In
your great essay "Place in Fiction" you say in talking
about the novelist and his duty that "the measure of
this representation of life corresponds most tellingly
with the novel's life expectancy." Do you remember
that in its context?

Welty: Yes.

Jones: "Whenever its world of outside appearance
grows dim and false to the eye, the novel has expired."
Do you think that the outside world has grown dim in
any of your work?

Welty: I hope not, but it's not for me to say about my
own work—that would probably always remain clear to
me. I still hold with that idea: this was a remark the
essay made about the writer's craft. I was referring to
the *novel's* outside world, the world of appearances, in
which the fiction takes place—not the actual outside
world. The novel's outside world, if well enough
created, does live on, when you look at the world of
Jane Austen, Flaubert, Turgenev, Tolstoy, Proust!
They're indelible. *War and Peace* is not only real to
today's reader, it will outlast him too.

Jones: What about this argument I've heard expressed:

"The world that Miss Welty is writing about in her work up through *Losing Battles* is dead for the most part; at least it's dead as an inspiration for novelists." Do you think that's accurate? I don't think it's fair.

Welty: Meaning the society is dead?

Jones: Yes, and even the interpersonal relationships.

Welty: Oh, no, I don't agree with that. I can't agree with that. The last things that will ever change are personal relationships. Society changes, of course, but human beings never have. I've heard people say that there's no such thing anymore as the family unit—well, I don't agree there either. We know it's still strong in the South. That's just rooted in our character, for the time being anyway. I think those things persist. Physical aspects could change in the society, but not the human qualities—belonging to Southerners and everybody.

Jones: You have also said that you think writers write on the same subject all their lives. Do you still think that that's true?

Welty: I don't know how specifically I meant that. I suspect I meant it in the most general sense. For instance, personal relationships will probably always be my subject, no matter how circumstances alter. That is what interests me and instructs me.

Jones: One final one: From the mid '60s when Frank Hains identified you as Mississippi's foremost literary figure and Jackson's most illustrious citizen until this minute you've been praised and received the kind of total adulation that very few heroes, much less artists, receive in their lifetime. I don't mean to embarrass you. Is that too strong?

Welty: I'm so overwhelmed and thrilled by all of this. It's much more, of course, than I ever deserve. Mississippi has been so good to me. In fact, elsewhere too. I have been truly lucky all my life, not only in my family and my friends but the people who turned out to be my editors and agents and almost everyone I've ever been connected with professionally. Somehow it has come my way that they have been just the very best and the most sympathetic. It's incredible.

Jones: It's because you're worthy and you've earned it.

Welty: No, I do work hard, and I like to do a good job, but you could do that all your life and nobody might ever bat an eye. You know that's true. It takes a lot of luck and I don't know what combinations of luck for something like that, a book's success, to happen. I know the chances. I'm grateful. It has helped me so much in all my work to think that at the other end there are people who are interested. That has meant so much to me, to have editors understand what I'm doing. There have been plenty of writers who've never had anything like that happen.

Jones: You tend to be a little bit better than most.

Welty: You can't tell. You can't tell. I still have a feeling—my agent Diarmuid Russell used to say when he was having such a hard time selling my stories, he said, "I believe anything that is a piece of good work is going to surface. It won't go forever unpublished." He said he'd believed that all his life. Well, of course that gave me courage. It may be true. I don't know. I hope so!

Jones: What has the creative life that you've led—has it cost you anything, in personal terms?

Welty: Well, I suppose so. It has given me more than it has cost me. Well, of course I work very hard. I don't count that as a cost. I love writing. I don't count that as a minus, I count that as a plus. But what has cost me is buying the time to work in by other means, you know, like lecturing or writing assignments and book reviews and so on. That's something I'm doing instead of fiction. I sometimes think I will never see the end, you know, that I can never stop. I've been working for the last couple of years to buy some time. Now for the present I don't need to because my book has made some money, but I didn't know it was going to. You know. Earning a living is a very big question mark when you are a writer. You don't know how, when, where, or if. It's just part of it, and you try to allow for it by doing things that are cash down on the barrelhead. And that has cost me in work of a different kind, travel and wear and tear. I like young people, and we get along, or seem to. I enjoy it, but it drains me. I don't always have enough energy left over to do my writing. But that's not a complaint. I'm just trying to answer your question. My writing life has given me so very much more than it cost.

Jones: It is not equal to what you've given us. I say that seriously.

Welty: I really love to work, to write, and when—it's my own fault—I don't manage the privacy or the time, it upsets me. I get so behind. I mean, look at that table. Every table in my house is like that. This one was just like that until just before you came. I thought you were going to put your thing up here. My conscience hurts me, you know, guilt, unanswered mail. But I'm going to deal with it. I have to.

Jones: Today one of the staff members at the Archives was taking a group of high school seniors around the building, and she took them up onto the mezzanine and showed them the Chinese translation of *A Curtain of Green* and said, "Here's a book written by Eudora Welty in Chinese," and one of the girls piped up and said, "I didn't know Miss Welty could write in Chinese!"

Welty: That's what I feel when I see them. I feel so proud. To think I could do that!

Jones: Write in all those languages.

Welty: I know it. That's wonderful.

Jones: Well. Let me tell you how much I appreciate your doing this.

Welty: No, I enjoyed it. I'm glad we got to talk.

Jones: Yes, ma'am, I am too.

Welty: I must say I thought all your questions were thoughtful and serious and sympathetic.

Jones: I'm just glad I got the opportunity to meet you and talk with you.

Photograph courtesy of the Memphis *Commercial Appeal*

Shelby Foote

ප

August 16, 1979

One of his first things he said to me when I arrived at his home in Memphis was, "I don't do these things very much," but he granted me two afternoons with him in his study. Both days I sat on an ottoman by some cardboard boxes containing a typed, unbound draft of the third volume of his *The Civil War: A Narrative*—with which, he said, he built his fires—while he rode a swivel chair at his desk. He wore bedroom slippers and khaki slacks, and kept his hands in constant motion loading and lighting, relighting and cleaning his pipe. Occasionally he would reach high into his bookshelves for a crumpled pack of Chesterfield Kings. The small pictures of Union and Confederate leaders and the passages of dialogue or official communication among them printed on note cards were absent from the wall above his desk, signaling his return to fiction. Both his voice and his thin face, covered by a thick, close-cropped gray beard, had the distinctive character of another era. I found it difficult to separate him from the deep traditions of which he spoke.

Jones: This is John Jones with the Mississippi Department of Archives and History, about to interview Mr.

Shelby Foote. Today is Thursday, August 16, 1979,
and we're at Mr. Foote's house in Memphis, Tennessee,
on Parkway. I suppose it's best if we start at the beginning, if you could tell me some of your early background, when and where you were born.

Foote: Well, I was born in Greenville, Mississippi, at
the Greenville Sanatorium on the seventeenth of
November, 1916, in room 31 although it was room 13.
They don't have room 13s in hospitals, I guess. The
doctor was Dr. A. G. Payne. My daddy was working
for a gin down in Rolling Fork and came up on a
freight train when he heard my mother had gone into
labor.

Jones: What did your daddy do?

Foote: He didn't do anything until after he got married. He was sort of a rich man's son that never thought
he would do anything in this world. About the time he
got married, his father lost all his money. My mother's
father, Morris Rosenstock, got him a job as a shipping
clerk with Armour and Company there in Greenville.
That was about 1915 or so. He just suddenly caught
fire and he lived another seven or eight years. By the
time seven years were up he was manager of all the
Armour and Companies in the South. But he died in
Mobile, Alabama, in September of 1922.

Jones: So your mother raised you?

Foote: Yes. I was not quite six years old when he died
and my mother never remarried. She did indeed raise
me. We lived back in Greenville until I was—well, to
get it straight, while my father was alive we lived in
various places because he was rising up the business
ladder. We lived in Vicksburg, Jackson, Pensacola, and
he had just been transferred to Mobile at the time he
died. He got a promotion each time. He'd had a good
life. He was born in 1890, a planter's son. He was
more interested in hunting and gambling and drinking
whiskey and fooling around than he was in anything
else, until he and mother got married.

Jones: Born at Mount Holly?

Foote: No. He was born at Mounds Plantation near Rolling Fork. He's buried there now. He lived at Mount Holly through his boyhood. My grandfather had three or four plantations down there. There was Mount Holly, Mounds, Egremont, and one called Hardscrabble. My Daddy grew up with that kind of life. His father had come from Macon, Mississippi—this is Huger Lee Foote I'm talking about, my father's father. His father was Hezekiah William Foote from Macon, Mississippi, a wealthy man there. He had been a Colonel in the Confederate army, was at Shiloh—in fact, got the tail shot off his horse at Shiloh. My father never had any intentions of doing anything with his life, so far as I know, until he and my mother got married. He did not go to a university. He went to Brannam and Hughes to school, and when college time came around he wasn't interested in that; he didn't go, he stayed around home. By the time he would have been a junior or senior in college he was getting married.

Jones: So your grandfather was the first Foote in the Greenville area?

Foote: Yes, he was the first one. He was the youngest son of old Hezekiah William, and his father sent him to Chillicothe Business College up in Ohio. I still can't imagine some Southern boy going to Chillicothe Business College. But his father sent him there—to learn bookkeeping, I suppose, and that kind of thing—and then sent him over to the Delta to manage four plantations. Mounds Plantation was one, where my father was born, and another was Mount Holly where they lived soon after that. Mount Holly was his favorite of all the places he was running for his father, so as soon as he began to run those places he began paying his father for Mount Holly. He wanted to buy it from him. He made the last payment the year the old man died, and then it was left him in his will.

Jones: I've heard that story.

Foote: That's hard.

Jones: And who gambled it away?

Foote: He did. He finally sold Mount Holly and moved to town and spent all his time gambling, some at the Elks Club there in Greenville, but he also went many places. I've talked with old men who knew him in poker games all over that region. He died of apparent cancer. I'm sure it was cancer; I'm not sure whether it was stomach or intestines or what it was. I remember them telling me he was sitting on a pillow during the last of his poker playing days. He also had one of the first operations that was known as the Murphy Button; something to do with an intestinal bypass. It was a daring technique in those days. My mother has told me about seeing him. He died a year before I was born. She told me about seeing him, but when she knew him best he was already in the hospital, lying up in bed there. My first novel *Tournament* is written out of sort of a conception of him, but it's only a conception. It's not even founded much on fact. I'd never seen him, I'd never talked about him a great deal with his widow or my mother, except for small things.

Jones: Was the Foote family always centered in Mississippi? When did they come down to this area?

Foote: They were originally in Virginia, went from there to Chester County, South Carolina, and from there across Alabama to the black prairie region of Mississippi, where my great-grandfather settled. He was, I've heard, the first man in Mississippi to bring in blooded cattle, to raise pedigree cattle. There's no trace of him left around Macon, no kinfolks even. I go there every now and then; I like to see the old man buried in the cemetery there—he's got an obelisk over his grave, and his four wives are buried around him, one to each of the four main points of the compass.

Jones: Is your mother still in Greenville?

Foote: She died ten years ago but she lived there nearly all her life.

Jones: Are there any of your close relatives in Greenville?

Foote: I have an aunt, Elizabeth Foote. I have another aunt, Katherine, her older sister, who's paralytic and in a nursing home in Greenville, and that's all.

Jones: What about the governor in the 1850s, Henry Stuart Foote, is he related?

Foote: He's a distant cousin, not close kin.

Jones: Where was he from?

Foote: Well, it's rather confusing. He's really a Tennessean. There is a connection though, he and my great-grandfather were among two of the founders of Vanderbilt, so they were connected that way. I don't know the exact kinship of old Hezekiah William to Henry Stuart Foote. Henry Stuart Foote's an interesting man. He was sort of a renegade. He left the Confederacy and went abroad.

Jones: Did he?

Foote: Yes. He was a fiery man, something of a blowhard, I think, and a mortal enemy of Jefferson Davis's, before the war and during it.

Jones: Had a fist fight with him, didn't he?

Foote: Yes, it was at a boarding house in Washington. He made a remark that Davis took exception to, about a young lady or something. Those fist fights never amounted to much; like any two fifty-year-old men swinging away at each other.

Jones: Well, he was quite a duelist in his time too, wasn't he?

Foote: Yes. You never know how serious those things are. There's a scene of him in the Confederate Senate, or House, I've forgotten which. He was attacked by a fellow member, a man named Dargan, I believe, from Alabama, with a Bowie knife. Foote managed to scramble out of the way, and some of the other Senators grabbed Dargan and pinned him to the floor, and Foote came back within range and said, "I defy the steel of the assassin!"

Jones: When you were growing up in Greenville, was your family literary?

Foote: No, my family was not literary on either side. I've done some speculating about that and there are several answers to where the devil the literary thing came from. So far as blood goes, and kinship, if it comes from anywhere it comes from my mother's father who was born in Vienna, Austria, and left there when he was seventeen years old and came to this country, probably to escape conscription; we don't really know why because he wouldn't talk about it. He was a Viennese Jew. His name was Rosenstock. He came over here when he was seventeen, and how he got to Mississippi from probably landing in New York I do not know. But anyway he came down the river and settled here and was keeping books on a plantation at Avon for a man named Peters, who was a planter there at Avon. This man Peters had a redheaded daughter who was a true belle, a beautiful woman. I've got some of her trinkets, and my grandfather married her. How a Jew bookkeeper managed to marry the daughter of a planter I don't know, but he swung it somehow. He had three daughters by her and she died bearing the third one. My mother was the middle daughter of the three. The oldest one had a great influence on me because I loved her very much and she was very fond of me and we were close. Her name was Maude. The younger daughter was named Minnie, and I suppose strident is one of the kindest words you can use to describe her. She's still living in Nashville, I think; a dreadful woman. My mother—I couldn't say too many nice things about her. She supported me in every sense all my life. A lot of bad things happened to me and she stood by me through all of them. She got discouraged I'm sure from time to time, but she never reproached me for any of my mistakes. I could see her disappointment. But she never said what I would have said in her place: "There you go again.

You're always acting like this." She never did that. The best way to describe her attitude toward me, and it's by no means a complete description, is that she never once hurt my feelings. It is a very strange thing to be that close to someone and never hurt their feelings. I hurt her feelings many times, in anger, in scorn. But she never hurt mine, though she had plenty of reason to.

Jones: What did she think about your work?

Foote: She liked it, and she was happy that I had found what I wanted to do. She would have been happy no matter what I'd done, if I enjoyed doing it.

Jones: At what age do you think that the notion of becoming a novelist and writer came to you?

Foote: It came to me, thank God, not too soon. I was editor of the high school paper there in Greenville, *The Pica,* it's called, so that I suppose I had some literary pretensions. But it didn't interfere with my life before then or even at that time. It took over my life later on. I lived a very normal Delta boyhood in spite of an interest in books. Incidentally, my first interest in books ran from *Bunny Brown and his Sister Sue* through *Tom Swift* up through *Tarzan.* So I've always been glad that I enjoyed dances and helling around the Delta. It's where I got much of the material I use now, so that I'm glad that I didn't become a recluse. When I got to be about sixteen or seventeen I discovered good reading and found out there was another whole world I had scarcely suspected up to then. The real thing that happened to me, I can almost pinpoint it, was when I was about twelve years old. For some reason or other, not having anything to do with school, I read *David Copperfield.* I had done a lot of reading of what I suppose can only be called trash. But reading *David Copperfield* I suddenly got aware that there was a world, if anything, more real than the real world. There was something about that book that made me realize what art is, I suppose, translating now. It made a tremendous im-

pression on me. I didn't then and there rush in to read
the rest of Dickens nor fan out into reading other
things, but it was the first real clue I had as to the
existence of this other world. I had a delayed reaction to
it because I was about sixteen or seventeen before I
came around to really reading. When I did finally come
around to it, for the next five or six years I read quite
literally almost everything I could get my hands on,
especially modern things. I heard somewhere, probably
from Will Percy, that the most important three novels
of the twentieth century were Thomas Mann's *Magic
Mountain,* Joyce's *Ulysses* and Proust's *Remembrance of
Things Past.* So, the first few months after my seventeenth birthday when my mother gave me the Proust, I
read those novels because I considered that I should
read them. It was a great time; I was like a colt in
clover with that stuff. It was marvelous. That's what, if
anything, made me a writer. The other strong influence
was the Percy family. I remember I was about fourteen,
something like that, out at the country club, swimming, and Will Percy came over. He'd been playing
golf—he was a dreadful golfer, but he liked to play
occasionally in those days—he came over and said,
"Some kinsmen of mine are coming here to spend the
summer with me. There are three boys in the group
and the two older boys are about your age. I hope you'll
come over to the house often and help them enjoy
themselves while they're here." I said, "Mr. Will, I'll
be glad to." That was the first I heard of Walker,
LeRoy, and Phinizy. Soon afterwards they arrived and I
began to go over to their house and they began to come
over to my house, and we became good and close
friends, which we have been ever since.
Jones: I have read that a lot of people think that the
fact that there wasn't ever a lynching in Washington
County, and the fact that the Klan never gained a foot
in the local politics . . .

Foote: Yes.

Jones: And even the fact that Hodding Carter could come there and write freely his type of journalism, was due to the atmosphere that the Percy family created.

Foote: There's a lot of truth in that, but there are other factors. The Percy influence was the main current sociological bar to the Klan. They set a style and an adherence to truth and justice that the Klan could have no part in, and people subscribed to that, so they had a high example in the community to go by, to guide them. They had other things too, though. Jews had always been prominent in Greenville. I was amazed to find anti-Semitism outside of Greenville in the Delta itself and, of course, elsewhere in the country. I was amazed to hear that Jews couldn't belong to the country club in Greenwood. I didn't know what to make of that because there were more Jews than any one religion in the founders of the country club in Greenville. It surprised me greatly. That, too, was a factor. Jews were among the most prominent people in town. If anybody knew Jake Stein and they heard somebody talking anti-Semitic they knew how absurd it was because they knew what a fine man Jake Stein was, and others too. It never caught on. But the Percys must not be under-rated in their influence in that fight. Senator Percy was strongly anti-Klan and expressed himself so at every opportunity. Mr. Will as a young man did what he could in that direction, too. In *Lanterns on the Levee,* he tells about the election that was held and how the Klan candidates were defeated. There are still some prominent men in Greenville who were members of the Klan, and old citizens know who they are and don't feel too kindly toward them to this day. It was not really as horrendous a thing as it sounds now. The Klan was political, almost social. I don't think that they intended to lynch anybody or put anybody in ovens or anything like that. Most of the members of it were politicians who were looking for bloc votes.

Jones: I heard you say on the ETV "Climate for Genius" series that had Mr. Will and the Percy family lived in Greenwood, then that would have been the place where the literary renaissance took place.

Foote: Yes. Well, now, that's something else. As to my becoming a writer—I said how I got interested in books on my own and everything else—well, Mr. Will had a lot to do with that, too, because he was something quite rare. He was a very good teacher, not a teacher in the sense of lecturing you, though when he got to talking it was very much like lecturing, sometimes. But it was by example. Here was a man who was a world traveler, who was widely read, who knew about the cultured forms of life on other continents, who had experienced the company of some of the fine writers of our time, and he would talk about it in a way that made you not only know the reality of it, but also appreciate the beauty of present day literature and past. I've heard Mr. Will talk about Keats, for example, in a way that made you wish the conversation would hurry up and get over so you could go home and read some Keats. He had that effect on you when he talked about it. He was a great admirer of Browning, too, which I am to this day, partly because of Mr. Will's influence. He had some blind spots, some serious ones with regard to modern literature. He had a low opinion of Faulkner, and he didn't think John Crowe Ransom was much of a poet. They had gone in a way different from his, so he didn't follow them. Surely he was wrong on that. It is a shortcoming on his part not to have been able to see the excellence of Faulkner and Ransom. But what he did like he could make you see why, and make you like it too. He didn't have any literary influence on me, his writing didn't influence my writing, but he was a marvelous example of a man who had availed himself of what good literature has to offer; not only literature, but also music and the dance, painting. He had been almost everywhere and seen almost everything. He was one of the few people I knew who before the war, the Second World War, had been, for example, to Japan and lived there for a time, and loved it very much, crazy about the Japanese.

Jones: But his character was one which was very affecting, wasn't it?

Foote: Right. He had a capacity for great anger. You mustn't think Mr. Will was all sweetness and light. He could get as mad as anyone I've ever known in my life. When the boys and I would get into some kind of trouble and break something—once we broke a fine Venetian chandelier. It was Roy's job to go down and inform him that the chandelier was broken, and I went with him. Mr. Will had a law office down at the Weinberg building in those days. We went down to the law office and stood around—we were about seventeen, I guess—and waited for Mr. Will to come out. He came out and Roy said, "Uh, Uncle Will, that chandelier in the library, I'm afraid it got broken." Mr. Will said, "What do you mean 'it got broken?'" It turned out that I had put some tennis balls in it and the youngest boy, Phinizy, had to turn it to get them and it unscrewed from the thing it was fastened to and came crashing down. Mr. Will said, "Goddamnit, people who don't know how to take care of good property shouldn't be allowed around it!"—just furious. Roy and I were scared to death of him. I don't know exactly what we thought he was going to do, but his anger was a fearsome thing to be around.

Jones: All the boys felt very close to him?

Foote: Absolutely. Sure. They called him Uncle Will and you see a lot of people referring to him as their uncle. He was their second cousin, their father's cousin. Their grandfather and Mr. Will's father had been brothers; that was the relationship.

Jones: What type of effect do you think that Will Percy and his writing has had on Walker?

Foote: That's an interesting question, because Mr. Will's values are not Walker's values. Walker would find the old Grecian, Roman stoicism perhaps admirable as broadsword virtues, but he doesn't think that's the path to heaven. He would have no satisfaction in it as a solution to what makes a man or what makes his soul. He would find some admiration for those qualities in a man as to character, but as to what made him really a man, Walker would find those unsatisfactory. That's partly because of the difference in their ages. Certain things were satisfactory fifty years ago that no longer are. The attitude toward the Negro, for instance, takes some understanding. Mr. Will, and Senator Percy before him, believed that the best thing any man could do was do his best in his circumstances and be a shining example, I suppose you'd call it, to the people around him. Therefore, the Negro's solution to his oppression and its various problems was to excel in spite of them so that when he made a claim for decent treatment and fair treatment, it had to be respected because of his excellence. That's basically the Booker T. Washington view: "Let your buckets down where you are." By the time Mr. Will came along, people were beginning to see that that might be a pretty good rule for the world at large, but it's not a good rule in a country where all men are supposed to be equal from the outset. A man is not supposed to have to prove he's equal in this country. That was one of the flaws in it. The other was that some of us poor souls are not equipped to do what superior men like Booker T. Washington can do. And it's a dreadful thing to see the government itself passing laws discriminating against you. So this solution of individual excellence was not a satisfactory solution, and Walker would never have found it so. Senator Percy now, before Will Percy, Will

Percy's father, he came at the end of his life, as a result of political failures—he lost any popular election he ever ran for—to believe that, as he said, "Shooting at the stars had always seemed to (him) to be pretty poor marksmanship." A man should succeed in his own area. Take his own little postage stamp piece of the country and be a good man inside that, and he would have done what he was put on this earth for. How much of that is sour grapes I don't know. I do know that he enjoyed his term as a Senator back in the days when he was elected by the Legislature, and I'm sure he would have liked to have gone on with that. And I think that this late view about "shooting for the stars" is an expression of his disappointment more than anything else, although it was his outlook at the end of his life. I remember Senator Percy, but only vaguely. I remember him as a dignified gentleman with a white mustache playing golf mainly out at the club. I remember his wife, Miss Camille, a marvelous woman, had a deep voice, very likeable. But they were dead a couple of years before the boys came.

Jones: Yes.

Foote: Yes.

Jones: He died in 1929.

Foote: Was it that early?

Jones: Yes.

Foote: Yes.

Jones: Walker is the oldest brother?

Foote: Yes, but he's only about a year older than LeRoy, a year and a few months.

Jones: And then how much younger is Phinizy?

Foote: Phinizy is about two years younger than LeRoy, maybe two and a half.

Jones: You were good friends with Walker all the way through college?

Foote: We went to Chapel Hill together.

Jones: Yes.

Foote: Then he went on to medical school at Columbia.

Jones: Did you finish at Chapel Hill?

Foote: No, I only went two years. I knew by the time I had been up there about six weeks that I didn't want a degree or anything like that. So I just took what courses I wanted to, and by two years I'd had plenty of it. I've always been glad I didn't stay.

Jones: And at that time you had decided that you wanted to write?

Foote: Well, I certainly hadn't decided I wanted to do anything else. Nobody every really decides he wants to write. I think I knew that, and aside from jobs in mills and cotton gins and things like that, all the other jobs I'd ever had were as a reporter or something like that.

Jones: At this time did Walker have any idea that he might write?

Foote: He was intent on becoming a doctor, but he was writing. He wrote poetry, both of us wrote a good deal of poetry back in those days and you can go back in the files of *The Pica* and read some of it I'm afraid. But, yeah, we were both writing, and when I got to Chapel Hill I wrote for the *Carolina Magazine.* Walker was so busy getting his science degree that he didn't have much time, but he too wrote a few things for the magazine, reviews of books and general articles on the movies, things like that.

Jones: Knowing Walker like you do, what do you think of the characters he's created: Binx Bolling, Will Barrett, Dr. Tom More. . .

Foote: Well, my judgement of Walker's work is really interfered with. When I read Walker I can hear him talking, and I know some of the stories he's told and some of the experiences we've had together that went into the books. He's not an autobiographical writer in the ordinary sense of Tom Wolfe, of somebody like that, but he does use things out of his life. I read him;

I'm a great admirer of his work. I think he's a substantial artist of our time.

Jones: I've read in an article or some place where he said, "You can be sure that I didn't learn to write by sitting at the feet of old men on the front porch listening to them tell stories."

Foote: Right.

Jones: How would you rate that influence on you?

Foote: I would rate it highly. I learned a great deal from listening to old men on the front porch, and so did Walker. He just meant that writing is not something that is picked up out of the air—which, of course, it's not. But he didn't mean by that to slight his material. The material was there for him and he absorbed a great deal of it listening to people talk.

Jones: When did you write for the *Delta Democrat-Times?*

Foote: I never really worked for the *Delta Democrat-Times.* I worked for the *Delta Star.*

Jones: Before they merged.

Foote: Hodding Carter came to Greenville and started the *Delta Star,* and I was a reporter on the *Star.* It was Hodding himself who worked harder than anybody, unless maybe it was his wife Betty who worked harder than he did, and then Donald Weatherbee was the managing editor who worked very hard, then I was the reporter who did not work very hard.

Jones: This was after you got back from college?

Foote: Yes, right after. One of the reasons I didn't go back to school—the main one was I didn't want to, but there was another one—was that the war was heading up in Europe. We all saw it coming. When it started in September of 1939 I joined the Mississippi National Guard, knowing that we'd be put into federal service pretty soon. We didn't go into federal service until November of '40. But during that year I was in the National Guard at home there. We met once a week and went to summer camp, and I knew I was biding my time until we went into service. I was very much in favor of our getting into the war because of Hitler. It was during that year that I worked mostly at the *Delta Star* and I also wrote the first draft of my first novel *Tournament* at that time.

Jones: It seems like your experience as a reporter has affected you, it comes out in your writing—*Follow Me Down.*

Foote: Sure, it would. *Follow Me Down,* for example, is an attempt to show the reaction of a town to a crime of passion, including the court trial. There were such crimes and I attended many such trials, as a reporter and just as a spectator. So, yeah, all that goes into it.

Jones: Was there any factual base behind *Follow Me Down?*

Foote: Yes. There was a man named Floyd Myers who drowned a girl named Emma Jean somebody, I've forgotten her name, and was tried for it and did get life imprisonment at Parchman. That was merely the basis for it. They didn't live on the island or anything like that, but he did drown her in Lake Ferguson there at home. There was that much to it. And I did attend his trial, which I learned a lot from.

Jones: What about the Parker Nowell character?

Foote: He's based in part on a lawyer named Ben Wilkes who was Myers's lawyer in that case, only in part though. Ben Wilkes didn't have a wife who ran off with somebody else. He certainly didn't listen to any thousand dollar phonograph and all that kind of thing. But Nowell was in part based on him. Nobody uses a real character entirely on his own in a book. You use parts of four or five people to make a character. And so I did with Parker Nowell. Nowell's phonograph, for instance, belonged to Mr. Will, which, incidentally, Mr. Will could never operate. He had less mechanical ability than anyone I've ever known in my life. He

couldn't operate an automatic pencil. Walker and
LeRoy and Phin got together one Christmas. He liked
to listen to the radio, but he never could operate one.
So, push button radios came out about 1936 or so. It
had push buttons on it for getting the different sta-
tions. Below, where the push button was, there were
celluloid tabs that a light shown through, and you
could take a pencil and write WQXR or whatever on
the little tabs. The boys showed him how to operate it,
said, "All you have to do is push this button and that
shows you the station." They came in the next day and
he had used a pencil and pushed the pencil through the
little celluloid things. He could never operate anything. He couldn't drive a car. He could never operate
anything mechanical. He was funny, faced with a mechanical problem.

Jones: He was a small man physically, wasn't he?

Foote: Yes. You didn't think of him as small, but he
certainly was, just as you didn't think of Faulkner being small and Faulkner was smaller than Mr. Will. Mr.
Will would make personal judgements against artists.
He didn't think they were exempt from the rules that
required you to be well-mannered. Faulkner came over
there once in the late twenties, I guess it was. Mr. Will
had a tennis court in the back there, and he took tennis
pretty seriously. It was the one sport he really did take
seriously. Faulkner had been drinking and got out on
the tennis court and made a fool of himself. Faulkner
never had Mr. Will's admiration as a writer or a man or
anything else after that display on the tennis court; he'd
shake his head about it every time he would remember
it. He didn't think anything good could come from
anybody who would do a thing like that.

Jones: Were you at home when Mr. Will died?

Foote: I was at officer candidate school at Fort Sill,
Oklahoma, and I got a leave, a furlough, just before I
went there. I was a sergeant in the 114th Field Artil-

lery and I got to go to officer candidate school, and on
the way there I got to spend a few days at home. Mr.
Will was in the hospital dying then. I had seen him
earlier when his health had started failing. He had an
ailment known as aphasia. His words would jumble up;
he would mean to say one thing and say another. Sometimes what he said didn't make sense. He spent that
last year in great distress, I now realize. He seldom
dressed—he would usually have on a dressing gown. I
can remember seeing him standing around—it was only
when I came home on weekend leaves and things like
that—but I remember being with him there one day
and he said something, and I laughed. He said, "You
mustn't laugh when I make mistakes, I have an ailment
that makes me make those mistakes." It is very sad to
me. It was a tragic death, in a way. It's especially
poignant because a couple of years before that, before it
ever hit him, he told me once he thought the worst
death any man ever died was Maurice Ravel, who had
just died about that time, and Ravel had aphasia. He
said the particular horror was that Ravel's thoughts, as
he understood it, were quite clear, but he could not
express them. He could think music, but he couldn't
write it down or play it on the piano. And that seemed
to him like a particular hell on earth. Then within two
years—I think Ravel died in '37 or '38—a couple of
years after that there was Mr. Will going through what
Ravel had gone through and what he described as a
particular hell on earth. It was very sad. He died while
I was at Fort Sill. I remember getting a telegram from
my mother about his death in the spring of '42.
Jones: Was he suffering that illness when he was writing *Lanterns on the Levee?*
Foote: No, he had finished *Lanterns on the Levee.* He
wrote *Lanterns on the Levee* on big, yellow legal tablets,
and his secretary, whose name was Mitchell Finch,
typed them for him. He, of course, couldn't have be-

gun to type anything. He wrote it in pencil on these
yellow sheets and Mitchell Finch would type them up
for him. I remember he got me to read a couple of the
chapters that he was particularly delighted with. They
read to me, in those early drafts, like he was finally
writing down what he had been telling us for so many
years, and they were not as effective written down as
they had been verbally, orally. But when I saw them in
print I saw how good they were. But in that form,
typed, except that they were pretty close to the exact
way he phrased things talking, they didn't seem as
good to me. Then when they got in print I could see
how good they were. *Lanterns on the Levee* is a beautiful
book in many ways.

Jones: Yes, I think so.

Foote: It is, however, a plea for and a summation of
the conservative position, and, as such, it's not hard to
discredit it. Many of the evils that I grew up with are
defended in that position, and would never have been
corrected with that position. The most persuasive thing
about it is his gentleness, his honesty, and his fairness.
I don't mean to shortchange any of those qualities in
him. They were all there in as full force as in any man
I've ever known. But I think most of us can see now
that men in those days didn't really address themselves
to the problems that were on hand. A thing that people
might not know about him though, if they took him
simply as some stereotype conservative, was his insist-
ence on respect for Negroes at all times. I remember
once I was over there sitting out in the living room
reading and the doorbell rang and I went to it and there
was a black man standing there, rather well-dressed and
everything, and he said, "I've come to see Mr. William
A. Percy," and I said, "Just a minute." I went back—
Mr. Will was in his study back there—and I said, "Mr.
Will, there's a nigger out here to see you." Mr. Will
looked at me real hard and said, "Tell Dr. so-and-so to

come right in." I had not meant anything by it, just a Mississippi boy talking, but he was quick to correct me on that kind of talk. And quite right. But he was closed off from anything he might think of as radical. Langston Hughes came down home and was addressing one of the Negro church congregations there, and the minister, who had known Mr. Will and Mr. Will liked, asked Mr. Will if he would introduce him. Mr. Will said he'd be glad to. So he went down there and it was an all-black congregation and Mr. Will introduced Langston Hughes as a fellow poet and an admirable writer. And then Langston Hughes, with Mr. Will sitting there, made what Mr. Will could only think of as a communist speech, I guess, or something. Anyway, he was furious at having been drawn into introducing a radical like Langston Hughes. Of course, Langston Hughes was not a radical, but he sounded radical to Mr. Will. I guess Hughes wanted people to stand up and demand their rights, and Mr. Will wanted them to earn them. I keep making it sound like he was a dark, double-dyed conservative. In some ways he was, but he was not looked on as a conservative by the community. They thought Mr. Will was practically a "mixer," as they call them nowdays. They didn't think it was right that he would receive Negroes in his home and discuss seriously the sociological and other problems with them. That was looked on as a pretty wild thing to do in those days.

Jones: He looked upon Negroes and the aristocracy as the true inheritors of the Delta.

Foote: That's right, that's right. There was nothing really unusual about that view; Faulkner expressed it sometimes. He said, "The white people have already lost their heads; it depends now on whether the Negroes can keep theirs." Oh, yeah. Their virtues, to Mr. Will, had almost nothing to do with freedom, it had to do with dignity, and suffering injustice in a better way than most people can. It would take a lot of thinking about before you would presume to sit in judgement on Mr. Will's views, but they are the views of the people who created a system that had a great deal wrong with it.

Jones: I sometimes feel that what Mr. Will was, Walker is working against.

Foote: Well, that's right; he is. But he's working against what's wrong with it. He's still admiring of what is right with it. I guess the best example of Mr. Will himself in Walker's fiction is in *The Moviegoer*. The aunt in that expresses the virtues Mr. Will believed in, and Walker obviously, at least Binx Bolling obviously, sees the inadequacy of those virtues. That's one of the things the book is about.

Jones: Your earliest influences were Proust, Mr. Will, and who else?

Foote: Certainly William Faulkner. *Light in August* was one of the first current novels I read. It came out around 1932 when I started reading earnestly. I read *Light in August* and I was tremendously impressed by it, and also puzzled by it. I've never written a letter to an author saying how much I liked his work or didn't like his work, but I had a very strong inclination to sit down and write Mr. Faulkner a letter saying, "You had such a good story to tell, why didn't you tell it instead of confusing me the way you did?" I've always been glad I didn't write that letter.

Jones: Did you come to know him?

Foote: Yes. I was with Faulkner maybe five, six times; spent the night in his house once, took a trip with him up to Shiloh once, had dinner with him and Miss Estelle a couple of times. I liked him very much. He was a friendly, even outgoing man with certain reticences. His reticences never bothered me; I figured a man with that big a genius strapped to his back would be bound to have some pretty hard times.

Jones: But you didn't see any great incongruities in him?

Foote: No, I didn't. I've read where other people did; I didn't. He seemed like William Faulkner to me, man and writer. I did not find any gap between the two. The man wasn't as great as the writer, but I'm sure that's nearly always true of great writers. I simply liked him. He was a good companion, a likeable man, a great deal of humor, a gracious host, and seemed like a fine husband—which I later found out he was not. But I liked him.

Jones: It seems to people, especially in my generation, the things that are taught to you about him are all rather dark concerning his personality.

Foote: Yep. Those things are rather hard to judge when you are young and a person's reputation is not overwhelming at that point. You'd just see him for what he was and you liked him or you didn't like him.

Jones: Was he interested in the Civil War, too?

Foote: Yes, he was interested in the Civil War, but only in an amateurish way. He didn't know much about it. Faulkner was never interested in the facts, the hard background, statistics, any of that. But he had a very fine if somewhat romantic view of the War, and he knew the general shape of it far better than most so-called buffs. He had a real good eye for terrain. I walked him over the field at Shiloh, surely one of the most confusing fields of the War, and he caught on to it fast. And I don't think he had ever been there before.

Jones: We talked earlier about how old people, sitting around talking and telling stories that even I still hear, influenced you a great deal. Were there stories passed around in your family about the War?

Foote: No; very few. I only saw about two or three Civil War veterans in my whole lifetime, and they had probably been drummer boys or something. Not much talk about the War. There were certain things left over

from the War. There were old maiden aunts whose
sweethearts had been killed in the War. There were
widows of Confederate soldiers around; they'd married
the old men when they were fairly young and the men
were old. There were customs that were very much a
part of it, although you didn't realize them too well.
For example, we never celebrated the Fourth of July
because that was the day Vicksburg fell. I remember
there was one family—it was very unusual to have out-
siders, even in Greenville in those days—but there was
a family there from Ohio and on the Fourth of July they
all got in their car and went up on the levee and had a
picnic and they forgot to set the brakes and the car
rolled down the levee and fell in the river. Everybody
said it served them right for celebrating the Fourth of
July.

Jones: Confederate history is something that has just
always fascinated you?

Foote: Yes. I read background material on the Civil
War at certain phases of my life the way other people
read detective stories. It did fascinate me. The actual
mechanics of the battles and everything interested me. I
wanted to find out what happened. And certain people:
Stonewall Jackson, Bedford Forrest, Robert E. Lee, interested me. I wanted to know about their lives. I
would read biographies of them—Henderson's *Jackson*
was one of the first that drew me to it, and Robert Self
Henry's *Story of the Confederacy* was an important book
for me as a young man, a child, really.

Jones: When you were in the Second World War, did
you have combat experience?

Foote: No. I was in the Fifth Division, a regular Army
division, and we were stationed in Northern Ireland
during the training period for the year leading up to
the invasion. I had a serious run-in with a colonel in
my battalion, and out of that a serious run-in with the
general of the whole damn brigade, and as a result of

their watching and waiting they jumped on me for
falsifying a trip ticket about a trip to Belfast and
brought me before a general court-martial, and I was
dismissed from the Army for falsifying a government
document. It was a real con job. What happened was
they had a rule that you could not use a government
vehicle for pleasure beyond the range of fifty miles, and
our battalion was fifty-two miles from Belfast. The
other two battalions were inside the circumference. So,
we commonly changed our trip ticket to forty-eight
miles instead of fifty-two. Anyway, that was the thing I
was charged with. It was just a simple con job. I came
on home, worked for Associated Press for about three
months in New York, and then joined the Marine
Corps. I was in the Marine Corps a year, including
combat intelligence school at Camp Lejeune, and then
was in California waiting to go over when they dropped
the bomb, and I got out on points. I had plenty of
points because I had four years in the Army and a year
in the Marine Corps. I was a captain in the Army and a
private in the Marine Corps. The other Marines used to
say, "You used to be a captain, didn't you? You ought
to make a pretty good Marine private."
Jones: It would seem like you had some combat experience just because of the way you write so vividly
about the Civil War battles.
Foote: Well, the Army experience itself was very useful to me. I learned a great many maneuvers of all
kinds, and I did study hard the use of artillery and
tactics.
Jones: Tell me the story of how you came to write the
trilogy. Originally it didn't start off to be that, did it?
Foote: No, it started off to be a short history of the
Civil War. Random House wanted me to do it and
Bennett Cerf was happy about it and I signed a contract
for a short history of the Civil War. It was going to be
about 200,000 words, not a long book at all. But I

hadn't any more than started before I saw I wasn't the
one to write any short history of the Civil War; just a
summary of what happened really didn't interest me.
But I was enormously interested in the whole thing.
So, about the time I got started—in fact, I hadn't done
much more than block out what I call the plot—when I
saw it was going to take a lot more space than that. My
editor at Random House then was Robert Linscott, a
very nice man, and I wrote him and told him I'd like to
go spread-eagle, whole-hog on the thing. It must have
been a terrible shock to him, but he saw Cerf and
whoever else he had to see and made his recommenda-
tions; they considered it, I suppose—I never heard any
of that; he just wrote back and said, "Go ahead." So I
did. What was really upsetting to them, this was supposed to be the first volume in an historical series they
were going to do: one on the Civil War, one on the
Revolution, and so forth. This first one turned into a
gigantic trilogy, so they didn't try any more.

Jones: Immediately you saw how enormous your task
was going to be?

Foote: Yes.

Jones: And at that time did you realize that you were
going to put your fiction down for twenty years?

Foote: No, I had no idea. I knew how big it was going
to be, but I thought I could write it fast. I thought it
would take me two years instead of one to write a
volume. Actually, as it turned out it took me five years
each on the first two and ten years on the third.

Jones: And did you put down your fiction during that
time?

Foote: Absolutely. I've never in my life been able to
do but one thing at a time.

Jones: What were your sources, besides the *Official Records?*

Foote: Well, as you say, the *Official Records* were the
main thing, but my sources were probably not over

250, 300 books. And I didn't use letters or things like that, manuscript stuff. I stuck to printed material.

Jones: Where did you get the insights that made it a narrative?

Foote: From learning how to write novels.

Jones: Is that right?

Foote: That's exactly what it is. Novelists know instinctively not to do things that historians do all the time. It's what makes historians such poor reading, and I'm not talking about being entertaining, I'm talking about what makes you dissatisfied with an historian, a dry, unskilled historian's history. There are great historians, I'm not talking about them. There has never been a greater novelist or writer of any kind than Tacitus, for instance, who was a great historian by any standards; Gibbon, Thucydides. It's just that a lot of modern historians are scared to death to suggest that life has a plot. They've got to take it apart and have a chapter on slavery, a chapter on "The Armies Meet," chapters on this, that, and the other. There's something almost low-life about trying to write about events from a human point of view. So they say. The result is they have no real understanding of the Civil War because they don't understand what Lincoln's problems were. They don't see them as problems impinging on a man; they see them as theoretical problems. I'm not saying what they do has no validity; I am saying it has no art. Of course, without their work I could have done nothing. They get along without me very well, but I couldn't get along without them.

Jones: Regimental histories, I've heard you say, played a large part.

Foote: Yes. They are not to be trusted for facts, but they are to be greatly admired for incidentals: how soldiers felt, what they did, sometimes humor, which is a necessary ingredient. I sometimes think that there's never been a single page of very great writing that did not have humor in it. It may be dark humor, it may be sardonic, it may be this and that and the other, but there's always humor in any good writing. There's scarcely a passage in Shakespeare that doesn't have humor in it, even if it's just a crazy juxtaposition of two words.

Jones: In your opinion, has history overrated or underrated any figures from the War?

Foote: Absolutely. The underrating of Jefferson Davis is almost like a giant conspiracy. Davis was a warm, friendly, outgoing man. When you read about him in history he sounds like a cold-blooded prig. It is almost unexplainable. It's just hard to believe how this gigantic conspiracy got formed, because some very fine historians think of Davis as a stiff, unbending man. He was not, not at all; he was the opposite of that. I just think, somehow, they don't pay any attention to things like his letters to his wife or those things, his fondness for his children. They would begin to question those things if they understood better the kind of man he really was.

Jones: Do you feel like he made the largest contribution to the Confederate war effort?

Foote: No, I wouldn't say that. Robert E. Lee is certainly a rival in that regard. He was the hardest working man in the Confederacy, I think—Jefferson Davis was. I agree with what Lee said; he said he didn't think anyone could have done a better job than Davis did, and so far as he personally was concerned he didn't know anyone who could have done as well. Davis had his shortcomings; he was too testy in his dealings with men like Joe Johnston and Beauregard. But I agree with Lee that, in sum, he did a better job than anybody else I know would have done.

Jones: What about on the Union side, who do you think was the most important individual?

Foote: Well, in this case there's no doubt at all because

Lincoln was. But Lincoln was a genius. He was a true political genius, and those are rare. It's one of Mr. Davis's misfortunes to be compared to Lincoln. Almost nobody can be compared to Lincoln.

Jones: Do you think Davis had the foremost intellect of his time?

Foote: No, Davis was not even an intellectual, though most people think he was. He was not. His tastes were really quite simple. In poetry his favorite poet was Robert Burns, who is a good poet, but certainly not of heavy intellect. He had little humor, too little humor, far too little humor, although he had more than most people realize. No, Davis had determination, will, and enormous integrity. If he gave a man his word there was no way he could be persuaded to go back on it. Lincoln would break his word to his best friend on earth, in two minutes, if it would help the Union cause to do it. And he never kept his word beyond the point where the conditions under which he gave it pertained. His enormous flexibility, his pragmatism, were incredible.

Jones: Do you think Davis could have served the Confederacy better as commander of the Mississippi troops?

Foote: No, I think Davis was right where he belonged. I've never been satisfied that Davis would have been a first-rate soldier. He was too intelligent for that, if you see what I mean. A good general ought to be a little stupid, to keep from getting rattled. There was a genius on the Confederate side all right, but it wasn't Davis or Lee, it was Bedford Forrest. I once told General Forrest's granddaughter that I had thought long and hard about these matters and I had decided that there were two authentic geniuses in the Civil War; one was her grandfather, Bedford Forrest, and the other was Abraham Lincoln. There was a pause at the other end of the telephone. Finally she said, "You know, we never thought much of Mr. Lincoln in my family." She didn't

like that coupling, that comparison, at all, and didn't
think much of me for making it.

Jones: What about individuals in the war who were
overrated?

Foote: Well, there are a lot of those, but it's hard to
know who is doing the overrating and does it matter
and all that.

Jones: Yes.

Foote: There are generals I don't like personally; Joe
Johnston's one of them. Phil Sheridan's another. But I
don't say from that they were overrated, it is just that
they had flaws that rubbed me the wrong way. I hope I
didn't let that show in the book, though I'm sure it did
to some degree. A historian has a great fondness for
scoundrels. Edwin Stanton was a scoundrel, but he's
very useful to me. He livens a page, picks it up. So too,
just as there can't be any good without evil, he makes a
good contrast for some other people who wouldn't show
up as well if you didn't have Stanton to compare them
to.

Jones: What about the notion that the North fought
the War with one hand behind its back, do you think
that's accurate?

Foote: Yes, I often say that, and I think it's quite
true. In the course of the War, the North passed and
acted on the Homestead Act. They developed the West
while the War was going on. Incredible inventions
were made during the Civil War—wars always bring on
inventions—but things that you don't think of like the
fountain pen, or the machine that sewed the uppers to
the soles of shoes, were made where one person could
do the work of forty people. There were many things
like that. Some of our finest institutions of education
were founded during the Civil War: Vassar, M.I.T.,
and a lot more. My point in this is that the North was
doing all those things and fighting the War at the same
time. If they had had to do more to win the War, they

simply would have done a great deal more instead of these other things they were doing. The Confederacy put close to everything it had into that War, but the North, as I said, fought it with one hand tied behind its back, on purpose. And they got rich in the process—selling their wheat crop to England, for instance.

Jones: So to think that the War was lost at Vicksburg, or the War was lost at Gettysburg, is completely erroneous.

Foote: If I had to pick any one point at which I said the War was lost—and I never would—I would say Fort Donelson.

Jones: In '62.

Foote: Yes, way early; February of '62. It did about four different things: it caused the loss of Tennessee and Kentucky—in the sense that Kentucky was never going to be recovered. It led to the isolation of the Transmississippi. Above all, it marked the emergence of U. S. Grant, the man who was going to win the War. But Donelson was reversible at Shiloh, except they didn't reverse it, so that you slip back and say, "No, Shiloh was the decisive point," and then, "No, if we had done this at Gettysburg," and you keep on with these might-have-beens and you wind up nowhere. I think the truth of the matter is there was no way the South could have won that war. The one outside chance was British recognition, and help, and we were not going to get that, especially after Lincoln defined the War as a war against slavery. The English people would never have put up with their leaders taking them into a war that had been defined on those terms.

Jones: But isn't it true that there was a point where England and France, especially Napoleon III who had recommended it, were considering intervention?

Foote: Napoleon III wanted to intervene for his own reasons, primarily to get Confederate cotton, I think, also to weaken a growing opponent, and perhaps some

political maneuvering to get England involved so that
strength could be drawn off that way. But the high
point that is often pointed to in recognition is a British
cabinet meeting that went on about the time the Battle
of Sharpsburg, or what the Union people called Antie-
tam, was being fought. When the results of that
reached England, Lee was in retreat and the time had
passed when they could have recognized them. But I'm
not at all convinced that if Lee had been successful in
that invasion the British would have recognized and
engaged in the War. That was a big step they weren't
about to take. You have to remember certain conse-
quences to England if they had come into that war. The
War of 1812 had wiped the British merchant fleet off
the seas, and the Northern navy would have done the
same thing in the 1860s. England wasn't about to be
crippled that greatly at a time when French power was
growing and the Germans were a threat from another
direction and all this was going on. There couldn't be
any kind of winner in that kind of thing. And the
English have never been famous for pulling anybody's
chestnuts out of the fire. They had general admiration
for the Confederates, but that admiration wasn't about
to be translated into terms of anybody going over and
fighting, or risking their fleet.

Jones: Even if things had worked out where Lee would
have won at Gettysburg and had gone down and taken
Washington, that, in your opinion, wouldn't have affected the ultimate outcome?

Foote: Well, it's problematical, of course, but not very
profitable to speculate on.

Jones: Yes. Today, do you still visit the battlefields?

Foote: Very seldom. If I happen to be close to one I
might drop by to see it. I get a particular satisfaction
out of doing it because I feel that it sort of belongs to
me now that I've written about it—all writers feel that.
But not much anymore. I've been determined to wash

the Civil War out of my head ever since I finished that
third volume, and I've pretty well done it, too. I don't
remember now where Stonewall Jackson was born.
Jones: Did you take President Carter around the
battlefield at Gettysburg?
Foote: Yes, and Sharpsburg and Harpers Ferry, all
three of them.
Jones: When was that?
Foote: July of '78.
Jones: Was he knowledgeable about the War?
Foote: Yes, not beyond the average good buff, but he
knew the War and was very interested, particularly in
what Georgia troops did—a natural thing, and likeable. I liked Carter very much; still do.
Jones: Was it hard for you to get back into the field of
fiction after twenty years on the War?
Foote: Writing is always hard work, but no, it wasn't
any harder writing *September September* than it had been
writing *The Civil War*.
Jones: Tell me where the idea for *September September*
came from.
Foote: I really don't know; it's not based on anything.
There was no case like that here or anything like it. I
wanted to get my hand back in by writing a short,
action novel; so I did. I researched it hard, the way I'd
done in history. The whole book takes place in the
month of September in 1957, which I could remember
because I was in Memphis, and I went down and read
the *Commercial Appeal* and the *Press-Scimitar* for the
month of September 1957, as a way of starting. I took
notes on what the temperatures were and how much
rain fell on the various days, phases of the moon,
changes that have been made in the city since then. So I
wanted it to be accurate, but I always wanted that, in
my earlier books too. The headlines and things that are
quoted in *September* are right out of the two papers.
Jones: Seems like you have sort of mellowed from *Fol-*

low Me Down to *September September*. Both of them are
about a crime; yet in *September September* no one gets
murdered.

Foote: Yes. What's more, I have a lot more tolerance
of people's shortcomings than I had back in those days,
I think, because I've discovered a good many of them in
myself.

Jones: I personally enjoyed *September September* very
much.

Foote: I'm glad. I expected it to be a runaway best-
seller, which it certainly was not. Everybody always
thinks something's going to be a runaway best-seller.
I've been lately reading about Faulkner; he thought
Absalom, Absalom! was going to take off like a rocket. It
certainly did not. It came out about the same time as
Gone With the Wind, in the same year, anyhow. I don't
know whether Faulkner ever read *Gone With the Wind* or
not. He said, "No story needs to be a thousand pages
long!" I don't think he ever read *Gone With the Wind.*

Jones: I read once where a reporter had asked him who
he had been reading presently, and he said, "I don't
read my contemporaries," and walked across the room
and proceeded to tell some writer that their work was
directly related to this other writer's work.

Foote: Right. The only book I actually saw him read
was a book called *Bugles in the Afternoon* by Ernest Hay-
cox, a western. But he was an avid reader. I've talked
with him about other books, but that's the only book I
ever actually saw him read.

Jones: Let me ask you a pretty nebulous question that
I think has a lot to do with what your fiction shows.
What effect do you think the Southern defeat in the
Civil War has had on us and our ideology and our
character?

Foote: Profound effect. In the movie *Patton,* Patton
stands up in front of an enormous American flag and
says, "We Americans have never lost a war, and will

never lose a war as long as we keep our qualities."
Patton was from Virginia, and when he said, "We
Americans have never lost a war," I couldn't believe he
knew what he was saying. He had lost a war. Southerners are in close touch with some things that the rest of
the country doesn't know much about, and one of them
is military defeat. And it wasn't just defeat; it was
grinding defeat. Without being annihilated, very few
sides in a war have ever been trounced as thoroughly as
the Confederacy was trounced. We were really beaten in
that war; we were beaten far worse than the Germans
were in either of the world wars, for instance. We were
ground down into the ground, and then ground down
some more after it was over. Southerners who are at all
aware of their history—and even if they aren't it's part
of their heritage—are among the people on earth who
know best what defeat is, and it has a great deal to do
with the way we see the world. We are also thoroughly
familiar with injustice, which can be recognized at a
hundred yards from our treatment of the blacks over
the century, so that a lot of American ideals are bound
to sound pretty absurd to an observant Southerner who
has been in touch with the underside of the American
character. It's very important, the fact that we were
defeated in a war.

Jones: We've talked for about an hour and a half and
I've got more questions that I'd like to ask you, but I
think at this point it would be good if we either took a
break or I came back tomorrow.

Jones: This is John Jones with the Mississippi Department of Archives and History, back for a second interview with Mr. Shelby Foote. Today is Friday, August
17, 1979, and we are at Mr. Foote's house in Memphis.
Yesterday we touched on some things that I would like
to pick up on today. Following Faulkner's death in '62,
didn't you go to the University of Virginia as writer-in-
residence?

Foote: Not really. I've been truly writer-in-residence at Hollins College for one semester, and while I was at Hollins I simply went down to Virginia for four or five days and sat in on some question-and-answer things and gave a reading in one of the auditoriums. I was not writer-in-residence at Virginia though; I was writer-in-residence at Hollins. I don't believe in writers having much to do with college campuses, or intellectuals for that matter, but it was a way of paying my daughter's tuition at Hollins. I made enough money to pay her way through school, and that's why I did it. I also gave a series of lectures here at Memphis State, about eight or ten lectures, I've forgotten. That was to pick up eating money while I was writing the third volume of the War. The Hollins job I took sort of in between the second and third volumes.

Jones: What exactly does a writer-in-residence do?

Foote: He usually teaches creative writing; that's usually his job. But since I didn't and don't believe creative writing can be taught, I taught a course on the modern novel. It was funny, too. I had four or five novels, I've forgotten which; they were Hemingway's *In Our Time*, Fitzgerald's *Tender is the Night*, Faulkner's *The Hamlet*, and I wound up with George Eliot's *Middlemarch*, which is my favorite English novel and I claim is a very modern novel. But after I started teaching these girls, who were twenty and twenty-one—they were all seniors or graduate students—I realized that every one of those novels had been written before those girls were born. Time had really caught up with me. But a writer-in-residence usually sort of gives the students a chance to get to know a working writer. I suppose it had some value; my advice to them always was stay away from writers. But I enjoyed doing it. For one thing, I had very little use for the young people of the sixties. They were talking what sounded to me to be an awful lot of foolishness. For example, they

wanted to know if a thing was "relevant," and if it
wasn't "relevant" they didn't want to have anything to
do with it. It turned out that a lot of things that mean
the most to me weren't "relevant," like Milton and
Browning. That set me off. I also did not like their
music, any of it. I never thought much of social protest
in the forms they favored. I don't have any basic objection to blowing up buildings and things, but I don't
like a lot of spouting off and running around with rifles
lifted in the air and giving salutes and things. Those
were the prejudices I went there with. I was pleased to
learn that though I never lost my objection to any of
those things that I just listed, I did like the young
people very much; they were likeable in back of all I
considered horrendous. They were likeable people. So it
did me that amount of good. I still believe strongly
that a college campus is a dreadful place for a working,
creative writer.

Jones: You don't feel like you can combine academics
and creativity?

Foote: It might be done by somebody, but he'd have
to write about academic things, I would think—which
is not a very satisfactory subject for a novelist. The
main objection to it I had was a general sharing of
intellectual concerns. People would sit around drinking
all night long, talking about their work in progress,
which I never would under any circumstances do. I
can't imagine any writer talking about what he's trying
to write about. I once saw a very foolish criticism, I
think by Malcolm Cowley, of William Faulkner. He
was talking about the unevenness of Faulkner's writing,
that there was a good deal of erratic and even half-
baked stuff in Faulkner, and his prescription for Faulkner was that he wished he could have had intellectual
friends to talk with and then he wouldn't have had to
commit all that foolishness in his work, he could have
committed the foolishness in conversation with his

friends. I don't know whether it ever occurred to Cowley, but he could have also committed the nonfoolishness in the presence of friends. These people I got to know, I liked them personally, poets and people like that who were writers-in-residence—they certainly were not writing any poetry; they were making a living. A lot of them had a wife and two or three children and they had to make a living, I suppose. It's hard to turn down fifteen or twenty thousand dollars a year and a house to live in, but it's not any way to live when you're a writer.

Jones: Did Mr. Faulkner feel the same way about it?

Foote: Well, he did become writer-in-residence at Virginia for two years. I've always thought that Faulkner, by that time, had decided that he had done his work and deserved some rest and amusement. And he was a vain man, as indeed all of us are, and I think he enjoyed the adulation and the company of young people. There's another thing about Faulkner—once the Nobel Prize came along, the public moved to meet him with respect. Before that, he had been an object of contempt, especially in his own town. He got the reputation of being extraordinarily stand-offish. I've heard that once, in objection to something that happened after *Sanctuary* came out, people would drive into his gate and around the driveway and stare at him. He didn't like that; he thought it was rude. He put up signs telling them to keep out, but they'd come in anyway. So, one day he was sitting on the gallery having a drink, and this carload of tourists, I guess you'd call them, came in to stare at him. He jumped on the banister and urinated into the flower bed in full view of these people, and they took off in a hurry. But I think when people moved toward him in any genial way he was genial in return. I know that, because he knew that I wasn't interested in any secrets out of his private life, and if I had been interested I wouldn't have presumed to ask him about them; he knew that. In my relationship with him he was one of the most genial, outgoing men I've ever known—delighted to talk about his work. He had no objection at all to talking about his work, and I talked with him a good deal about it.

Jones: Do you think he resented the way the people of Oxford saw him? Going to school up there you hear all kinds of wild stories.

Foote: Yes, I think he did resent it, and he had every right to resent it. When I was a young man, back in the thirties, you'd be in Oxford and you'd ask directions on how to get to his house, and people would turn their heads to the side and spit into the street. They didn't like him being there, and they didn't want anything to do with anybody who wanted anything to do with him. It was that bad. Also consider some of the Tom Wolfe syndrome. Wolfe, you know, was told that if he ever returned to Asheville they'd lynch him. They wouldn't have, but they told him that. Well, some people in Oxford thought Faulkner's stories of miscegenation and all that kind of thing were giving the Glorious South a bad name, and they resented that. I never had much of that trouble. I had some general resentment by people that I didn't punch a clock, but that's about all it amounted to. Anything I did, like I had a big white boxer, weighed over a hundred pounds—I was very fond of him, he was with me all the time—a lot of people thought that was a total affectation to have this big white dog that you go around with.

Jones: Where were you living then?

Foote: Greenville.

Jones: Did you work on your trilogy when you were working at Hollins?

Foote: I've never done any work away from my home. I did do some research and take some notes and things like that, but I hadn't any more than started on that Hollins job, which I had agreed to, than my mother came down with cancer, and I had to commute between Hollins and here almost every weekend. She was in the hospital here in Memphis, and at home here too. She left Greenville and came up here to be with us during all this treatment. I had planned to do a good deal of work—I was up there by myself; my wife stayed here with our child—but because of my mother's critical illness during that time I didn't.

Jones: Was that the major reason you took ten years on your third volume?

Foote: Well, when I finished the second volume I thought I had another five years to go and I accepted this Ford Foundation grant with the Arena Stage in Washington as a sort of vacation, a way of resting up for starting the third volume. I enjoyed it. We got a townhouse in Georgetown with a swimming pool and all that. We spent Mr. Ford's money right and left. We were there about, I don't know, six or eight months, and it was very pleasant, and that six or eight months I deliberately used as a vacation. Following the Washington thing we had the brilliant idea of going down to the Alabama coast and building a house on the Gulf there. There were two things wrong with that: one, I got crossways with the Ku Klux Klan down there during the George Wallace days, and the other was we had an architect here in Memphis named Adalotte design a house for us. It was a three-story house with a nine-foot gallery all the way around the two top stories. It was a beautiful house; but we found that in a sixty-mile-an-hour wind it would fly. So we had a lot of delays on that, and finally decided not to build it.

Jones: What kind of pressure did you get in Alabama from the Klan?

Foote: It wasn't bad. It was the kind of pressure anybody would run into down there if he let it be known what his feelings were, different from theirs. They considered that their backs were to the wall and they even

translated themselves into terms of being modern-day
Confederates, which is what they were not, and I told
them every time I had any kind of confrontation with
one of them or saw them with a Confederate flag; I told
them they were a disgrace to the flag, that everything
they stood for was almost exactly the opposite of everything the Confederacy had stood for, that the Confederacy believed in law and order above all things. Its main
hope was to get in front of the courts, while they were
cussing the courts and wanting not to have anything to
do with them and wanting to disobey the orders of the
courts. I created a good deal of resentment against myself down there until they decided I was crazy and then
they were more sympathetic.

Jones: You've said you've spent the last five years or so
trying to wash the Civil War out of your head.

Foote: Yes.

Jones: Do you feel like your fiction is a more lasting
literary contribution?

Foote: I don't know how I feel about that; I don't
know that it is more lasting. It could be that I have
more pride in and affection for my fiction than I have
for my history because it all came out of my head rather
than out of documents. But I'm satisfied with that job I
did on the War; those three volumes suit me; I'm
proud of them, and willing to stand by them. I'm also
protective of the novels because most people think that
the history is my serious work and the novels are not up
to that standard. I disagree with that, violently.

Jones: Do you get more pleasure out of working with
fiction?

Foote: No, they're not that different, writing history
and writing fiction. All the same problems are there.
Somewhere in one of the bibliographical notes I said it
doesn't much matter if facts come out of documents or
out of your head, they are still things you work with
and respect. You are looking for the truth, and, as I

said also, it's not a different truth, it's the same truth.
You try and find out the truth, and it doesn't really
make that much difference—to the person writing it,
anyhow—whether you made up the facts, which you
then must respect, or you found them in documents,
which you must respect. I never felt cramped at all
while writing the history. I felt just as free as I feel
when I'm writing a novel. It's true, I couldn't make up
the color of a man's eyes, but I could find out what
color they were. It just meant a little harder work.
Jones: You didn't have any facts in the trilogy that
weren't completely documented?
Foote: Absolutely not. If the work didn't have abso-
lute historical integrity it would have been a total waste
of time. There would be no point whatsoever in doing a
novelistic treatment in the sense of inventing scenes
that would explain Robert E. Lee or how Stonewall
Jackson looked. All that has to come out of fact, and
the whole thing would have been vitiated if I had invented anything or distorted anything. It wouldn't do.
I've never known a modern historical instance where the
truth wasn't superior to anybody's distortion. I would
be willing for that book to be subjected to any kind of
iron rule about accuracy. If I didn't do that, I would
say that it was not worthwhile.
Jones: I was always fascinated by the incidentals in the
narrative. You knew exactly at what point Stonewall
Jackson was leaning up against a tree sucking on a lemon.
Foote: That's right. Those things are all in the documents. Nothing flatters me more than to have someone
ask me if I made up some scene, because I hope it
sounds as if a novelist wrote it, but I didn't make up
anything in it. I may have done some conjectures of
which I do very little in that book, and my interpreta-
tion of why somebody did something or the future
effect of what had been done in the past is a contribution, I hope. But any facts in there are facts, whether

it's the weather or the color of somebody's hair and eyes or his height and weight or his age or what his schooling was, what his voice sounded like; all those things are accurate. I'm not saying I didn't make some errors and mistakes, I'm sure I did. But they were as accurate as I knew how to make them.

Jones: What about when you were writing, did you read one sequence ahead in the *Official Records* or would you get a whole overall view and write from that?

Foote: I did a whole overall view, reread some of my favorite books, read other books that I had not read, biographies, general histories of the War, studies of individual campaigns, always the *Official Records of the War of the Rebellion,* that 128-volume monster. I read all that and that gave me the information with which to plot the whole three-volume work. Having done that and having straight in my mind how the plot was going, I then researched each individual incident as I came to it. I would generally research at night and write in the daytime.

Jones: But you could sit down and write the complete scene freehand?

Foote: Yes. I would have notes stuck up on the bulletin board for quotations or so I could remember what book something was in. I never had a typist or an assistant or a research person or anything like that. I did it all myself, and I couldn't have done it any other way. I couldn't have asked somebody to go find something in a book for me; I would have gone crazy waiting for them to find it, for one thing. And I certainly didn't want anybody turning out a whole bunch of notes for me, so I didn't want any kind of secretarial assistant. I didn't even want anybody typing it because that gave me another chance to improve it—each copy you make is that much better. But I would be sitting down writing a scene and I would remember something that happened and that somebody said something at that point; then I would scratch my head and remember what book it was in, and then when I went over and got the book I would remember that it was about two-thirds of the way down the page on the left-hand side, and I would find it. Sometimes I would be stopped dead cold in my tracks for two hours while I tried to remember what book and what part of that book it was in. But that was my way of doing it, and it suited me. Any short cut would have been an interference.

Jones: What about the criticism you got on the trilogy, was it mainly that you took too much of a Southern bias?

Foote: There was a little bit of that. There was some objection to winding up on the note of Jefferson Davis, for instance, as a continuation of this war against Jefferson Davis which was waged from 1861 to 1979, and will continue to be waged. There was a little bit of that, but to tell you the truth I saw very little criticism of anything about those books. It was all praise. There was no attack on it, almost none. I saw, I'd be guessing if I'd say, four or five hundred reviews, and practically none of them, some of them were lightweight and slight, but nobody really attacked it, said, "No, no, no." Some people were disappointed by the treatment I gave certain characters, favorites of theirs. I remember a very good historian named Vandiver had some objections to my depiction of Stonewall Jackson at the Seven Days, but that was just a difference of opinion; it was not a direct attack on any facts I had.

Jones: He said something about Stonewall Jackson delaying on the way to Mechanicsville or Gaines Mill?

Foote: He said that Jackson didn't delay, he did exactly what he was supposed to do.

Jones: Ordered.

Foote: Yes. Some truth in that, but it wasn't Jackson in his spread-eagle style, God knows. And Lee always wanted men to do more than they were told to do. In fact he said he learned from General Scott to bring the armies together, bring all his units together on the field; then the battle was up to them.

Jones: And you don't think you'll ever involve yourself in another novel or any type of history of the War?

Foote: I doubt it. Originally I thought I would do a short novel early in my writing life on a Civil War subject and that was to be *Shiloh*. I wrote that. Then in the middle of my writing life I hoped to do a big historical novel on the Siege of Vicksburg, and at the end of my writing life I wanted to write another short novel on the Battle of Brice's Crossroads, all of them basically Mississippi battles—Shiloh, of course, being just across the state line—but I won't write the Vicksburg novel and probably won't write the Brice's Crossroads novel; I've been there, you see. T. S. Eliot said an interesting thing that all writers know to be true. He said, it's in one of the *Four Quartets,* he said that writing—you're trying to do a thing that you don't know how to do, and, he said, it winds up a general mess of imprecision. Having done it you have learned how to do it, but having done it you're no longer interested in doing it again. That's the tragedy—if you know how to do it, it's because you've tried and bungled, but now that you've learned how, you are no longer interested because you wouldn't be learning. Many people think that writers are wise men who can impart to them the truth or some profound philosophy of life. It is not so. A writer is a skilled craftsman who discovers things along with the reader, and what you do with a good writer is you share the search; you are not being imparted wisdom, or if you are being imparted wisdom, it's a wisdom that came to him just as it came to you reading it.

Jones: That's a good point. Can you tell us something about other things you learned in writing the trilogy about the uniqueness of a Southern heritage?

Foote: I'll tell you a very simple thing that I got out of writing about the War that tremendous long time. It started at the very beginning and continued through the writing. I acquired a knowledge of and a love for Southern geography. It's great when you learn about the rivers and the mountains and the way the South physically is. That's a thing that is important to us. People do draw from their physical backgrounds. Whether you live in the mountains or on the seacoast makes a big difference in what kind of person you are. There are other things too. I'm from the Mississippi Delta which has a forty-foot top soil and is often said to be the richest farming land in the world—it's not, but it's often said to be—and I've known some people out in the hills too, and I've discovered that there's sort of an inverse ratio between the richness of the soil and the providence of the people who live on it. People who live down in the Delta don't worry too much about the future because the soil is so rich they don't have to, I guess. It's like Hawaiians; when they get hungry they can reach up and pull a pineapple off the tree. An Eskimo, if he stops thinking about food for two hours in a row, would starve to death, and so he knows to think about it and to do something about it. Out in the hills of Mississippi you'll see people canning vegetables and doing all kinds of things looking forward to a hard winter. Down in the Delta they just go down to the supermarket and buy a can of beans. It's funny. George Washington Carver, one of the finest men I ever met, came to Greenville in the early or middle thirties to lecture to a big Negro gathering there celebrating one hundred years of progress or something, and he reproached them something awful. He said, "I've seen Buick automobiles in the yard of a house where you can study botany through the floor and astronomy through the roof." He wanted them to be frugal and look after themselves; be good, solid citizens. Dr. Carver was a fine man. I remember his speaking. I covered it as a reporter on the newspaper there as a high school boy when I was working for the paper in the summertime. I remember one thing that made a great impression on me. First, Dr. Carver did. I've seen about five or six great men in my life, and Dr. Carver was certainly one of them. Another one was a psychiatrist named Harry Stack Sullivan who came down and visited the Percy family back in the thirties. But what I remember about the Carver visit was there would be audiences of five or six hundred people—it was in the very hot summertime—and every person in that audience was dressed. They all had on ties and coats, and they were very proud. They were all black, no white people there, or scarcely any. I remember how proud they were and they showed their pride through dressing up, and it was hot. This was Mississippi in July or August, I think, when there was no air-conditioning ever heard of. They were great in that respect.

Jones: Did Mr. Will bring him to town?

Foote: He brought Harry Stack Sullivan, but not George Washington Carver. That was done by the blacks at home there; they brought him over from Georgia. I guess after the death of Booker T. Washington, Carver was probably the best known Negro in the country, because of his work with what he called, "the lowly peanut." He was a wonderful man.

Jones: Who else did Mr. Will bring to town that had an effect on you?

Foote: Oh, I'm trying to think of the many people I met at the Percy house. I remember Roark Bradford was there one time, a very funny man, really funny. Dave Cohn stayed there at the Percy house for about a year writing a book. He came on a visit and stayed a year. He was from Greenville and he'd been in New Orleans as manager of Sears Roebuck or something. By the time he was a little over forty years old he figured

he'd worked enough and made enough money to live on
and he didn't want to be a businessman any more, he
wanted to be a writer. He came back home and went to
see Mr. Will about it, and Mr. Will said, "It's all well
enough to say you want to be a writer, but writers
write. That's what you have to do, not talk about it."
And Dave said he thought he would, and Mr. Will
said, "Well, fine. Why don't you stay here at this
house? You can get it done." Dave Cohn stayed there
and in less than a year wrote *God Shakes Creation,* probably his best book, and he wrote seven or eight more. I
like Dave Cohn's work. He had a good ear. He was very
good on blacks. He wasn't ashamed at all to see the
absurd side of them, which Roark Bradford had pointed
out so well by then. Dave was also interesting about
certain provincial aspects of Memphis. It was Dave in
God Shakes Creation who said, "The Delta begins in the
lobby of the Peabody Hotel and ends on Catfish Row in
Vicksburg." He was always welcome at the Peabody;
they were glad to see him—he stayed there whenever he
was in Memphis—but they never even gave him a cup
of coffee, and he thought it was rather amusing that
they had so little appreciation of this publicity. Any
New York hotel would have put him up and fed him
for years. The Pontchartrain in New Orleans would too.
But not in Memphis.
Jones: Reading that type of thing and Hodding Carter's work, you get a different sense of the Delta than
you do in your work. Your work is closer to Faulkner.
Foote: Yes; more influenced by Faulkner certainly.
The Delta is generally misunderstood. For some reason
we in the Delta think we are the aristocrats of Mississippi simply because we've had more money than most
other sections of Mississippi. At the time I'm talking
about there was damn little anybody had, but the Delta
was better off than other sections. And we thought of
ourselves as the aristocrats, with pure blood lines and

all that foolishness. Actually the Delta is a great melt-
ing pot—God Almighty's a big dollar mark. It's not at
all the way it's portrayed, say, in the work of Tennessee
Williams. I've never understood Williams writing
about the Delta when he had Columbus on the Tom-
bigbee River, which is a much better place to write
about than the Delta. What I mean is it is much better
for Tennessee Williams to write about Columbus because he knew it, and he didn't know the Delta. I've
always been interested—more than say Faulkner was—
in the actual historical shaping of a society, the events
which caused people to be the way they are, and their
conflict with those events. I'll probably never write anything past the mid-sixties. I kind of stopped looking,
about that time.

Jones: Are you going to return to Greenville in your
work again?

Foote: Yes. I'm writing a big long family novel right
now called *Two Gates to the City.* It's about a family in
the Delta. It's not an historical novel. It's about a
group of people, probably in the late forties. It's not a
saga by any means. It's a family novel in the same sense
as, say, *The Brothers Karamazov.*

Jones: What do you think is the truth behind the fact
that so many writers come from Mississippi?

Foote: That's a question that's often asked, and there
is no easy answer. There are good flippant answers, such
as there's nothing else to do down there, so you write.
There are only two movies in town so you haven't got
much to do. You go to court and watch a trial. My day
was before television, so that didn't take up an awful
lot of people's time. I've seen recently that the average
American boy watches something like six hours a day.
It's unbelievable. And you have to subtract that from a
lot of things, that six hours out of the waking eighteen.
You've got six of that and six of school and six eating or
something, you don't have much left for reading or

doing many of the things I did when I was a boy.

Jones: So you think something basic is changing?

Foote: Oh, yes, a lot of things are changing. I always hesitate to say it's for the worse, no matter how worse it looks to me, because I've heard these dithyrambs before from people saying it's a miserable damn time. When our leading writers were Fitzgerald, Faulkner, Hemingway and Dos Passos, people were saying, "There are no good writers around anymore; Dreiser's dead," and so on.

Jones: But do you see something changing in the Southern character?

Foote: I'm sure it must change. For one thing, when I grew up we had a peasantry. That being gone has a profound effect on things. Imagine Russian novels without a peasantry. Imagine Faulknerian novels without blacks. Well, sure it's changed. That's not necessarily for the bad though; we'll just have to wait and see. You're always at the mercy of history, of events, as to whether you have good writers or not. You can't turn them out by any formula; you can't provide a society that will result in good writers. In fact there's a curious paradox there. Our best writers have come out of dreadful times, and out of dreadful systems. Mozart and Beethoven, Bach and Haydn composed under what was largely a patronage system—the worst of all systems, supposedly, but it produced some terrific work.

Jones: I read in a 1952 interview that somebody did with you where you said that you didn't have any other hobbies, that writing was your religion. Is that still the case with you?

Foote: Yes, yes, I don't play golf or even poker. I don't belong to any clubs or anything; don't do anything but write.

Jones: Do you write everyday now?

Foote: Try to, yes. I'm a slow writer, 500 words is a good day, but I always worked seven days a week. I

don't do that anymore; I take off Sunday and I don't
work eight hours a day like I used to, I work five or six
hours. I've written and published over two million
words, and so if I'm tired I feel I have a right to be.
Jones: Who do you think that today is writing the
best fiction, besides Walker and you?
Foote: You mean for the whole country?
Jones: Yes.
Foote: There's some I like a lot. There is no one I
think measures up to the big men before our time,
certainly not Mailer or Styron or Capote, but there are
writers I like. I think John Updike is a skillful writer.
My favorite writer among people who have come along
after me is Cormac McCarthy; I like his work a great
deal. He had a new novel out about two months ago
called *Suttree* that I like a lot. That's his fourth book. I
like McCarthy's work very much. There's a South
American writer that I put off reading and finally read
about two months ago that I am really crazy about. His
name is Garcia Marquez. He wrote a book called *One
Hundred Years of Solitude*. It's one of the finest novels
I've ever read in my life, unbelievably funny. It's got a
huge, mythic sort of Faulknerian quality to it. I like it
very much. That book came out in 1970 and I didn't
read it until eight or nine years later. I called Walker
right after I finished it. I was so pleased with it, I said,
"Walker, Jesus Christ and God Almighty; I've discovered a very great novel!" He said, "Hey, what is it?"
I said, "It's called *One Hundred Years of Solitude* by Garcia Marquez," and Walker said, "You son of a bitch, I
did my best to get you to read that book five or six
years ago and you wouldn't do it." I'd forgotten he ever
said anything about it. It's a good book though.

There's a big gap in my reading of novels caused by
my Civil War reading. I read very few novels during
those years. I would go back and read *The Brothers
Karamazov* or *The Magic Mountain*, but I wasn't reading

modern novels, except writers that I was particularly
interested in like John O'Hara or Styron and Mailer.
Something has happened to writers in our time that's
very serious. When they get early fame they get torn on
the bias; they get pulled crossways. It's no easy thing to
be twenty-six or seven years old and be on the cover of
Time magazine and have people clamoring after you all
the time. You get to believing the extravagant praise,
you get to appearing on television talk shows, you get
to attending conferences and all that kind of stuff. I
don't know why they let themselves in for it, but it
appears to be unavoidable. There're some who have
managed to avoid it; Salinger steered away from it; but
he appears to have gone down the chute even without
it. I don't know. It's a hard time, though, because of
instantaneous communications and the tremendous
growth of television and that kind of thing. It really
gets at you. I'm certainly comparatively obscure; and
yet you wouldn't believe the amount of stuff that comes
into this house—people wanting me to read and comment on their novels or do interviews or write for travel
magazines, all this kind of stuff. And there's a lot of
big money flying around. I'm not surprised that a lot of
people are seduced by it. It's wrong. I have no idea
about what to do about it. There are pressures out of
nowhere, such as being writer-in-residence somewhere.
A young writer learning his craft has got no business
being a writer-in-residence. When I was coming up
there was nobody that wanted me on any college campus whatsoever, but now they want all these young
boys and a lot of them are on campuses and they're not
doing a damn thing but laying the coeds. It's a bad
scene, particularly for poets. Practically every poet you
know is on a college campus somewhere if he's under
sixty years old. It's had a bad effect, I think. He ought
to be out in the world, writing about what he sees out
there, not on a college campus. There are also all kinds

of grants and things that are very bad. I ought to be in favor of anything that would help my fellow writers, and me too. I've had three Guggenheims and a Ford Foundation grant, but they were for purposes of researching the War when I had to travel and buy books, which I'd have a hard time doing without Mr. Guggenheim's money and Mr. Ford's money. But I still think it's bad, particularly for young writers who are learning their craft. No matter how pitifully poor and small the living is that you earn with your pen, you get a tremendous strength by earning your living by your pen. If you're living off government money or grant money, you lose that, and it's a big loss. Now I'm talking particularly about a young writer. After you get a little soft in the belly and the head, I suppose such money doesn't do you much harm. But it diverts you from what should be your pride, it diverts you from what should be your concern. Wondering where your next meal is coming from is a splendid thing for a writer; it's not bad, it doesn't cripple him up, it doesn't keep him from working. Going out and having a job as a common laborer or a timekeeper or something like that is a hell of a lot better way to reinforce your income than teaching on a college campus. Writers used to know that. You can't imagine Hemingway or Fitzgerald or the early Faulkner or John O'Hara or any of those people doing any of those things. They simply did not do them. There was very little opportunity to do them, but they didn't do them. They knew it would interfere with their work, and they put their work first, not their wife and children.

Bagley: Do you think this can help at a later date? Miss Welty gives the W.P.A. credit.

Foote: The W.P.A. did fine work. That was some-

*Clinton Bagley, a former historian with the Department of Archives and History, is a resident of Greenville.

thing else. People were starving and people couldn't go out and dig ditches; there was nobody digging ditches or anything. The W.P.A. gave you just a little bit of money, enough to keep you from starving, and those people did some good work. But there, once again, I'm talking about major writers: Faulkner, Hemingway, and Fitzgerald weren't on W.P.A., they were home working. They didn't even have time to go down and earn a little bread to put on the table, they were busy writing. Some of those three were making pretty good money; Hemingway, for instance. But that wasn't their concern. Their concern was getting their writing done, and learning how to do it.

Jones: What about the future of the Southern novel? It seems like a lot of things we always thought of as Northern qualities have come down on us.

Foote: Yes, there's a good deal of homogenization going on. When you're traveling and stop in a Holiday Inn, you can't tell by the looks of the room whether you're in Minnesota or Mississippi. When you go into a restaurant to eat you can't tell where you are. Regional food, regional lodgings, all that is pretty well over. And so I suppose, as a result of radio and the jet plane and those things, we'll all be evened out more and more as time goes on. When I was a boy, people didn't know how to pronounce Roosevelt's name, they called him R*oo*sevelt (vowel sound as in shoot). It was double O, and they had never heard anybody say it. So you had strong regional characteristics simply because of a lack of communication with the rest of the country. I think the attempt to preserve a heritage—not as a brake on progress, but as a matter of pride in that heritage—is a very valuable thing and should be hugged onto. I approve very much of these latest things such as you're doing here, trying to catch the time and fix it with the use of tape recorders and various other things, and the preservation of documents that would be destroyed.

The Department of Archives and History there in Jackson has done some marvelous work on preserving things that would have been lost without it. But you can't have pride in your heritage if you don't know the heritage. I was driving through Mississippi, I think it was on a Monday, and I can't remember what year it was [1963], but I heard on the automobile radio that there'd been a bomb set off in a church in Birmingham the day before, and three little Negro girls had been killed. So I was going through a place called Prentiss, Mississippi, and I pulled into a roadside restaurant-cafe to get a newspaper to try to find out what had happened. I went in and the proprietor was standing behind the cash register talking to a Mississippi highway patrolman. There was a waitress down the counter there. I went up to the proprietor and said, "Do you have a morning paper?" and he said, "We're all sold out." I said, "I wanted to find out something if I could about this Birmingham explosion, a bombing or something in a church over there." He said, "Yeah, that was all in the paper this morning. I guess those niggers will learn sooner or later." I said, "Well, I must not have heard it right on the radio. It said three little girls were killed." He said, "That's right," and I said, "Thank you, anyhow," and went and sat down at the counter. The waitress came over and I said, "I just want a cup of coffee," and she went to get the coffee. I turned back around to the proprietor and said, "This town is called Prentiss,"—I've left out one thing he said. "We've got to preserve our heritage," was one of the things he said in the extenuation of this bombing and everything else; his notion that we had to hold the blacks down if we were going to preserve our heritage, because it would be destroyed. Anyway, while she was getting me the coffee I turned back to him and the patrolman and I said, "This town is called Prentiss; is it named for Sergeant S. Prentiss?" He said, "I don't know," and I said, "It seems likely, but it might have been some other family name, Prentiss or something." He said to the waitress, "You know how Prentiss got its name?" She said, "No, I don't know," and the highway patrolman said he didn't have any idea. That showed you how much their heritage meant to them. It was a strange business though. There's a log of ugliness down here. Yet I know from my experiences in the North and in the South that that same man, if I had been broken down on the side of the road with car trouble or something, he would stop, get the jack out of his car and help me, get all greasy and dirty, and would not have expected anything more than a "thank you" for doing it. It's a curious mixup of traits. Most of the evil comes from ignorance. It seems that the good is inherent and the evil is acquired. I have a candidate to blame for all this. I think the planter is the "nigger in this woodpile." He's the son of a bitch who set the system up so he could rule the roost, and he managed to keep everybody under him quiet by promising them about this open society where they could be planters someday and live the way he lived. Sometimes I'm amazed at his genius, at how well the whole thing was designed. Even the giving of Christmas presents to plantation workers was designed to demean them. Almost everything about day-to-day life on the plantation—and I speak with some knowledge because I come from a long line of planters—was designed to hold these people down so that he could live the way he did. I don't know if people would even believe it nowadays, but it was quite common for a cook who worked seven days a week, all day, fixing breakfast, dinner and supper, to make three dollars, three-fifty and four dollars a week. What she got for that was money, which she used to pay her house rent, usually about five dollars a month for the cabin she lived in with no plumbing, and cast-off clothes, and food to take home to her husband and

children at night. That can't be a good system. That's
bound to be a bad system. And the people who were
paying that to her, in many cases, were making a great
deal of money. Something was very wrong at the core of
it, not only in slavery days but in those days too, which
practically amounted to peonage. My grandfather and
two other men at home, including Senator Percy—it
was my grandfather, Senator Percy and O. B. Critten-
den—had a plantation across the river, where the
bridge goes now, called Sunnyside. They brought in
Italian and Sicilian workers; paid their passage over on
the boat. The three men nearly got into serious trouble
with the federal government because a Catholic priest
who was ministering to those people saw what was
being done to them. It amounted to peonage; they had
to work off their passage and it never worked out so
that they got clear. The three men were very nearly
prosecuted for peonage, but they managed to get from
under it by the fact that Theodore Roosevelt had met
Senator Percy as a young man when he came down to
my part of the country on a bear hunt with my other
grandfather. This was my mother's father who was in
on the plantation; his name was Rosenstock. My other
grandfather Foote had had Roosevelt down here on a
bear hunt, and they got to talking, "What are we going
to do when we're not hunting with President
Roosevelt? How are we going to talk with him? We'll
bore him to death." So my grandfather said, "We'll ask
Percy along; he can talk with him." So, as a result of
that relationship they were able to get the indictment
quashed, or anyhow not prosecuted on condition that
they let the people go.
Jones: Mr. Foote, I've kept you long enough. Before I
cut this off I want to say how much I appreciate your
talking with me. It's been an honor to meet you.

Photograph by Sam Tata

Elizabeth Spencer

🍂

August 10, 1981

She'd come back to Mississippi from her home in Montreal to attend the Faulkner Conference at Ole Miss, and to give a reading at the Old Capitol in Jackson from her newest book, *Marilee*. Before a substantial crowd in the House of Representatives, Miss Welty introduced her and she read "A Southern Landscape" and "The Day Before" in a soft accent unchanged by her years in Italy and Canada. Afterwards, as I waited for my chance to talk to her while she signed books, I overheard an older resident of her native Carroll County describing just how closely she resembled her mother, and how the county Miss Spencer had left in the 1940s had changed. The next day she called me to say that a motel was no place for an interview, and we agreed to meet in the Archives Building later that afternoon.

Jones: This is John Jones with the Mississippi Department of Archives and History, about to interview Miss Elizabeth Spencer. Mrs. John Rusher is how you're known in Montreal.
Spencer: Yes.

Jones: Today is August 10, 1981. We're at the Archives Building in Jackson. I've got a list of questions for you. Looking during my research on your writing life I wasn't able to find out a whole lot about your early background other than the fact that you were born in Carrollton, Mississippi, and the names of your parents. Can you tell me something about your early memories, your family, and that type of thing?

Spencer: I was born in Carrollton. My parents were both from Carrollton or from Carroll County. My mother, I suppose, was born at the McCain family plantation. My mother's family were the McCains. There were some military heroes in the family. There were two military leaders from West Point and two from Annapolis. My great-uncle was General Pinckney McCain, who was a general during the First World War. He trained the Allied Expeditionary Force which came under the command, I believe, of General Pershing.

Jones: Sure.

Spencer: Camp McCain at Grenada was named for him. Then my mother's brother William Alexander McCain, who went to West Point, I believe he served in both the Mexican Rebellion and the First World War, and later became head of the quartermaster depot in Philadelphia. He retired to Bucks County, Pennsylvania. And his brother, Admiral J. S. McCain, commanded the task force under Admiral Halsey during the Second World War. His son was another admiral, John Sidney McCain, who was in command of the Pacific fleet during the sixties. He retired about five years ago, and only recently died, as you may know. My mother, however, lived a very quiet life. Of her two younger brothers, she was—there were two crops in that family for some reason. There were my two uncles who were in military life, and a girl, Miss Katie Lou, who taught Latin for years at McComb, Mississippi, and was a very

highly educated lady. Then there was a long gap. I
think maybe two children died. Then there was my
mother and two other brothers. My mother, I think,
was the next to the last. Then my father was the
youngest one in his family, and I was the youngest one
in our family, so it happens that I was only two generations from the Civil War. My grandfather remembered
it though he was too young to go. My father's father,
who was dead before I was born, had fought at Gettysburg. So when I say that, that my grandfather was in
the Civil War, people look at me like I'm crazy, but it
really is true.

Jones: Right.

Spencer: Let's see. You were asking me about my parents. Well, my mother was born at Teoc—that was
what they called the plantation—in Carroll County. It
was a plantation near Malmaison which was Greenwood
Leflore's plantation in the Teoc country. Teoc Tillala
was the Choctaw name for tall pines. You may have
heard of that. Well, my mother was a very pretty girl
and she became a music teacher. That was one thing
open to young ladies. My grandfather was elected
county sheriff and moved into Carrollton, and she
moved up to McCarley, a little town near Carrollton, to
get what music pupils she could. That was the thing
one did: you lived with nice people who had a piano
and you taught music. She saw my father up there, or
rather he saw her. I think they went together for a little
while. Then he moved into Carrollton to start business
on his own, and they were married there and lived there
ever since. They bought a house there. I was born in
that house, and they both lived there the rest of their
lives. It was a long lifetime for both of them in one
place.

Jones: Yes. I'd read where your dad worked as a
farmer.

Spencer: Well, I don't doubt that he worked as a

farmer when he was growing up simply because they were very poor. It was right after Reconstruction in the 1880s that he was born. His father died soon after. They had farms and apparently had good houses and friends and everything, but it was just a hard life. His mother had to raise the four brothers. There were four brothers and a daughter that died. She had to do her best with those children. So he went one year to college and had to go back home to take care of his mother who was sick, and then they all got together, because she got tuberculosis, and they chipped in and sent her out to San Antonio to try to prolong her life. It went back a long way, but he remembered it just as fresh. Then he left McCarley. The Spencers at McCarley were C&G station agents, and Railway Express agents. They had a country store and the station, a whistle stop. They had a house and a farm. My father moved into Carrollton, and I believe he bought a store, but first he worked for the Railway Express in Carrollton. But sooner or later he started doing absolutely everything. He had stores for this and that. You know, anything that was going, he'd try it and make money at it. It cost a lot to raise us, I guess, and he knew he had to do more than one thing. He had the Chevrolet agency and the Standard Oil franchise, and he sent the Standard Oil delivery truck all over the county. I think my brother used to drive it in the summer time. And he had a cotton gin, and he had a little farm down in front of our house. In front of our house was a good many acres, about forty acres, on the outskirts of Carrollton.

Jones: Is the house still there?

Spencer: Oh, yes. We sold it to a family that descended from a family that had always lived in town, so I know it's going to be done right by.

Jones: And who in your family remains in Carrollton today?

Spencer: Nobody. Friends. In McCarley were my un-

cle and his son who moved to Greenwood, and for a
while his daughter, until she married and moved into
Memphis. They skipped Carrollton. They just jumped
from McCarley to Greenwood. We went to Carrollton
and never got to Greenwood. You know, a lot of
Greenwood was settled by Carrollton. Carrollton is in
the hills, but Greenwood is in the Delta and richer.
Jones: But you grew up with a strong sense of the
difference between hill people and Delta people?
Spencer: I was brought up on the margin of the Delta,
on what they call Valley Hill. Valley Hill can be any
road going down that last hill. There were many Valley
Hills. Just like that song about the Tallahatchie bridge.
Well, what bridge did she mean? Nobody really
knows. Any bridge over the Tallahatchie might have
been it. Those plantations dated back a long way, and
they were just on the margins of the Delta. Usually the
houses that were built—I know my mother's family
home that burned in the 1880s was built on the last
hill overlooking the Delta. It must have been extraordi-
nary. But their plantation was—you know, part of it
would be in the hills. But you get central to the Delta,
most of that was swamp, if you remember. It was just
dead things and swamp. Really ugly. All that's gone.
The trees are gone, all those big trees that used to stand
in bayous and swamps along the road. Most of that's
gone, as I understand it. I've just ridden over to Greenville this trip, but it looks to me like it's all been
drained and controlled. Where're you from?
Jones: From here. Jackson.
Spencer: Are you a lifetime Mississippian?
Jones: All my life.
Spencer: Where's your family from originally?
Jones: Yazoo County and the Delta.
Spencer: Yes. But the central part of the Delta is what
I'd think of as new country. Right along the river,
Greenville and those places, they were all old. The

central part of the Delta was dangerous. It was a very rich land if you could control the buckshot and the bayous and get the mules out of the mud. You had to get the cotton picked in the fall. Black labor was what it came to. But Mexicans used to come in to do that too. They were called wetbacks. It's just a whole different thing now from what it used to be. There was also yellow fever. Everything bad.

Jones: As Amos Dudley discovered in *This Crooked Way*.

Spencer: Well, that's the book I wrote about tales I'd heard about the people who opened up the Delta. People like that.

Jones: Fascinating book. Was there anybody in reality that you fashioned Amos Dudley after? Somebody in your family perhaps?

Spencer: No. He was an imaginary character. But I used to hear a whole lot of stories. I remember that what started that book off was my uncle sitting and talking one twilight down at Teoc. Somebody asked him about two brothers who'd gone over into the Delta and made what amounted to a lot of money at that time. Somebody said, "Where did they come from?" And he said, "Just like a lot of Delta folks, they came from out of the hills dragging a cotton sack, and in ten years they had a fortune." That sort of stuck in my mind. And I thought about, "Well, why did they leave home?" You know, there had to be some impetus. I had conceived of there being two brothers, just following what he said, but then as soon as I set up that scene, I realized it might be a man and his friend.

Jones: Arnie.

Spencer: Yes. And then Amos developed a strong personality of his own. His resentments were strong already, and he was caught up in the whole opportunistic thing of the Delta and its really primitive condition. See, he married a woman from near the river. I thought there would have been older families over there. The part he was opening up was very new.

Jones: A lot of people who talk about the phenomenon of there being so many writers from Mississippi, especially from the Delta, say that there was a compression of history, a great deal of drama and life packed into a very short period, that took place in the Delta, so that a family could go to rags to riches to rags often over one generation.

Spencer Yes.

Jones: They say that is great for a writer, for developing his sense of his time and place. Did that help you, that much being packed into one generation?

Spencer: Which generation do you mean?

Jones: Well, just in general over the two generations that cleared the Delta, the people who went from rags to riches like Amos Dudley, and the ones whose riches were lost.

Spencer: Who were ruined. No, that didn't affect my family. We were from Carrollton as I was telling you, and that's a hill town. I separate my father from a man like Amos Dudley. His ambition was to make a living for his family, to raise his children and furnish support. He was very conscientious, responsible about money, but money was just so hard to make. It was only in the last years of his life that he had any kind of affluence, modest though it was. He was always just struggling away trying to put my brother through college and then medical school, and then me through college. I went to graduate school one year, but that was all. That kind of syndrome of just fabulous gains from cotton land, and failure, largely depended on. . .I suppose unexpected crop failures might ruin people, or two or three bad years. But I don't think that in *This Crooked Way* Amos Dudley fell on evil times financially. Do you?

Jones: No, ma'am.

Spencer: I did hear stories about people going broke. "Becoming land poor," they said. They acquired more land than they could manage. Sometimes there would be accidents like that. I never personally knew anybody who went under that way. I know my mother's family plantation was always mortgaged, but I think it acquired the mortgage just after the Civil War. They probably had a large investment in slaves, and they couldn't sustain themselves after what happened. I just don't know how they managed the debt. But it wasn't until the 1940s that my father and my uncle got together and paid it out. They put it under single management rather than leave it divided property among the heirs.

Jones: Right. Tell me about your early life. You were born in Carrollton in 1921?

Spencer: Yes.

Jones: Can you tell me where the literary influence came when you were growing up?

Spencer: Well, I wasn't a very healthy child and Mother loved to read. She had extraordinarily good taste in children's literature, and also other literature. She came from a family that liked to read. I told you they had a plantation house that burned in the 1880s. They always said that they lost everything, but there were a great many books somebody had grabbed and got out with. Either that or maybe the library wasn't destroyed. There were Dickens and Scott, and then there were a vast accumulation of the things my uncles and my aunt had studied at college: Latin texts and histories and things like that. I don't think the McCains were literary or bookish people, but they made ready reference to books. They put great weight on education, like a lot of Scots Presbyterians do, and they were a strong Scots family—I think my grandmother was one generation from Scotland. I have heard that. I'm not quite sure that's true. She was from an old town that vanished, called Middleton. You might have heard of that. It was between Vaiden and Carrollton. It was a very thriving town before the Civil War. There was a shoe factory there during the Civil War to make shoes for the soldiers. They read an awful lot. I suppose my father's family had nothing against reading, but they probably had too tough a life to give themselves over to too much literature and music. I'm not certain of that. It may not even be true, but my impression was that. But among the McCains, you were supposed to read and talk about books. When I was sick a good deal as a child my mother used to read aloud to me all kinds of things: Greek and Roman myths. She was very strong on the Bible too, so she used to read Bible stories. Let's see, she read King Arthur's stories, Robin Hood and other childrens' books. Later on I became fascinated by all this, and as soon as I began to write in school I began to write down stories I imagined. I had a little black playmate. I knew far more blacks than I did whites when I went to school, because I used to spend a lot of time down at the plantation. Around the house the cook's children played with me. Our house was out from the center of town anyway. I used to make him listen to stories I'd made up. I think he was bored.

Jones: That's interesting, because certainly the kind of relationship a small white girl living on the fringes of town had with blacks in the '20s and '30s is something you have always investigated from "The Little Brown Girl" to "Sharon."

Spencer: Yes.

Jones: So listening to your mother read instilled in you an early love for the language?

Spencer: Oh, I think so. Some people probably have this naturally. I'm sure my brother was read to, too, but his bent wasn't literary. He was inclined to want to study medicine and scientific things. Since mine was literary, I had all that to catch on to. I kept on with it.

I got encouraged when I went on through school by the teachers I had who were also interested in literary things.

Jones: You came to Belhaven after graduating from Carrollton High?

Spencer: It was J. Z. George High School then. They consolidated some schools. J. Z. George was the senator from Carroll County who had brought Mississippi a new constitution after the Civil War.

Jones: Why did you choose Belhaven?

Spencer: I didn't! I liked Belhaven. I'm sure it is a good school. No, I wanted to go to the University. My family were all Presbyterians and they had ties with Belhaven, and they decided I should go there. So, I guess I counted my blessings that I could be given a college education. I think I got a scholarship there too. That was a little bit of a help. It was because I was first in my class.

Jones: Yes. At Belhaven did you have someone who took you by the hand and said, "You have talent. You could be a writer." Was it that early that you knew that's what you wanted to do with your life?

Spencer: I wanted to be a writer for a long time. I started writing stories when I was in grammar school. The teachers said they were really good, and they read them aloud to the class. I'm sure they weren't any good at all, but it was just the idea of having done this that was exciting to me. I used to sit up in trees and write. I would sit out by myself. It was a large property and there was a gully in back of the house and a steep fall of land. I used to sit back there and write in notebooks and hide the notebooks in some old machinery that had been dumped down there to prevent erosion. Then I wrote long stories and copied them in tablets and gave them to my mother and father. They were generally adventure stories about people getting isolated at the North Pole about which I knew absolutely nothing.

Crazy things like that. I must have picked up frag-
ments to put together in stories like that from books
and from magazines my brother had.

Jones: So even that early you knew?

Spencer: Yes.

Jones: It's interesting to me to talk with writers about
the first impulse to write.

Spencer: I can't explain it. I think there's something
chemical about it. I remember when I first got this
terrible urgency. I stayed awake all night with a kind of
excitement about something or other. There was a fire
in the room burning and casting shadows. The next day
I tried to paint that, I tried to draw, but I had no
talent for painting, so I wrote a poem. You know, it
was some way to release this inner excitement. I don't
think that's explainable. Mississippi doesn't explain it;
nothing explains it. Being read to as a child doesn't
explain it. It's a kind of chemical excitement you feel,
and you're drawn toward one sort of expression or
another. As I couldn't draw it, I wrote.

Jones: So you almost had to do it?

Spencer: I think so. I think some people have that
kind of urgency. But where it comes from, I don't
know.

Jones: Yes. You went on to Vanderbilt and studied
under Donald Davidson, a man whose name I've heard
many times. What about the academic training for a
writer? Faulkner and Shelby Foote disparaged it. Do
you think it's something every writer needs?

Spencer: I never took creative writing at Vanderbilt. I
know that was a center for writers. It was assumed in
the English department that it was more a center for
literary studies. It might, as a by-product, stimulate
writing. I really think that's what creative writing,
which I've spent so much time from time to time teaching—it's something I hardly believe in myself, except
that I think you can encourage and stimulate and direct

students. Sometimes it's your Christian duty to discourage, de-stimulate and defuse students. You just know that they're never going to write anything. Not everybody has to be a writer. It seems to me you should relieve them of the idea that they have to be writers. To my mind for a certain type of person it's a waste of time. Be that as it may, Vanderbilt—I didn't study creative writing there. I took a little creative writing course at Belhaven. We had a little club—like they had the French Club for students interested in French, and a Music Club, and we had a writing club.

Jones: That's where you first met Miss Welty.

Spencer: Yes. We decided to ask her over to the college. She and I both have told that story many times.

Jones: But what about the idea that a college campus is probably the worst place for a working writer, being isolated and stuck off away from life in the unreal world of a college campus?

Spencer: Well, unfortunately writers have to make a living, and universities have been marvelously generous in giving a place to writers. Writers-in-residence are not required to teach full time, and yet they are given good enough money so that they can exist and write. If they want to live off-campus it's generally all right, if they report for their duties. Sometimes the choice is like that. I suppose a writer doesn't have to take it. Nobody is making you be a writer-in-residence, or associate yourself with a college campus unless you want to. Faulkner chose not to. I was just reading a biography of Faulkner. I've never read a biography of Faulkner before. There's an excellent one out by David Minter, who was at the Faulkner conference, a man from Georgia. Faulkner apparently was given books that stimulated him a great deal by Phil Stone, and was exposed that way to a kind of education that, it seems to me, was maybe even better than taking one course after another in college. But he was certainly bookish

enough. He read a great deal. I've forgotten what our
original question was. About colleges and writers?
Jones: Yes.
Spencer: And continuing your education? Well,
you've got to get an education from somewhere if you're
going to write. I don't believe in unlettered, untutored
writers.It seems to me literature springs from literature. But whether you have the formal degree or not:
that's empty as far as your writing goes. Your writing
depends on the quality of the work—wherever it comes
from. Have you ever heard of an unlettered, untutored
writer who was a good writer? They might be good
storytellers, and if what they say is taken down it
might make what they call oral literature. There have
been attempts made at that. I think at Mississippi
Southern at one time they were drawing people in from
a rather wild part of Mississippi called Sullivan's Hol-
low. You may have been associated with that?
Jones: No, ma'am.
Spencer: But you know about it. I don't know if this
kind of thing transcribed makes for a true literary production. I'm just not sure. Certain untutored things
have great interest. Louis Rubin, who was at the Faulkner conference, he was talking about a diary of a family—let's see, post-Civil War, I believe, and I believe
either in Virginia or South Carolina—and he said, "It
reads like a damn novel." You know? It was just unbelievably rich and full of, oh, I don't know, lost currents
of emotion, violent relationships, this, that. I've forgotten the name of it. It's going to be published. I suppose
literature just springs up sometimes. Something like
that might be a great work. But I'm talking about the
general pattern now. I think that literature springs
from people who know about it, study it, read it, enjoy
it.
Jones: You were saying before we turned the tape recorder on that you went to Ole Miss from '48 to '53?

Spencer: I taught at Ole Miss.

Jones: Right.

Spencer: I taught '48, '49, '50. In '51–'52 I took off to finish a novel I was working on. '52–'53 I taught there, but in '53 I got a Guggenheim Fellowship, and I left.

Jones: At that time you went to Rome?

Spencer: Yes.

Jones: I wanted to get your impressions of the influence Mr. Faulkner had on you, if you ever talked to him about your work or his. *Fire in the Morning* came out in 1948, so indeed you were a published novelist living in Oxford too.

Spencer: I was introduced to him twice and I said, "How do you do, Mr. Faulkner?" and he nodded, and that was all. This was passing chance social acquaintance. When I got to know Faulkner best—it shouldn't really even be called an acquaintance—was in Rome, of all places, even though I'd lived in Oxford. I don't think he was aware much of me or my work. I think he knew the title of a book I'd written because he mentioned it in Rome, but he said he hadn't read it. But at that time when I was in Rome in '53–'54, somewhere along in there, he came. You could look it up. Everything's documented about Faulkner now. I don't think he ever went uptown for a sack of groceries without them finding out about it now and putting it in a biography. He was there in Rome. There was a very nice guy who was head of the Cultural Service named Fox, and he and Mrs. Fox had a very beautiful apartment in the Renaissance part of Rome near the Tiber, and they gave an evening party for Mr. Faulkner. Of course, he was a small man. He was standing there in the corner of the room with a glass in his hand, which he never referred to, and they said, "Come on, you must speak to Mr. Faulkner." And I went and said hello, and he did remember me and asked me how I

liked Rome and I said fine. Then someone else came
up. But after the party Allen Tate, who was in Rome
with his wife Caroline Gordon, asked me to go to dinner with them and Faulkner and another person. She
was a rather wealthy woman who was a novelist and had
a long car with a chauffeur. I suppose this was part of
the deal. We went to a nice Roman restaurant. Tate
talked to Faulkner most of the time. I was rather shy
around Faulkner. I knew that he was shy. I felt shy,
and I didn't want to talk to him. There's nothing worse
than trying to talk to somebody who doesn't want to
talk to you. Don't you think?
Jones: Yes, ma'am.
Spencer: So I was just in favor of leaving him alone. I
remember we came back together. There was a girl
with him named Jean Stein, I think. We came back
together in the chauffeur-driven car. Something was
said, because his hotel was near to where I was staying,
something was said about his coming to lunch. I don't
know who said it. He said, "If you will call me I'll
come." I never did. I don't particularly like to know
writers just to say I know writers. If they turn out to be
warm and companionable people—I mean, Eudora
Welty is a charming person to meet for dinner or to
have as a friend and to chat with. I just can't imagine a
more friendly person. But I would feel that about her
whether she was a writer or not. That's what it comes
to. Faulkner was strange and withdrawn from most
people, so I didn't want to intrude on his thought
processes, whatever they were. I met a good many people in Oxford that did have long friendships with
Faulkner. I knew Phil Stone very well. Phil called up as
soon as he knew I was in Oxford. He and Emily used to
have me over for drinks and we'd chat a lot about
writing. Phil talked a lot about "Bill" as he called him,
and what he thought of his work. He was a very good
talker, Phil, and an interesting man.

Jones: He loved Faulkner?

Spencer: Oh, I think they had one of those friendships you could call love or just lifelong devotion to each other. Maybe there were tensions. I don't really know. I think it was certainly a significant friendship.

Jones: But did his writing influence you as a young writer?

Spencer: Oh, I'm sure it did. I never did read Faulkner, in spite of the fact that my family read a lot and didn't exclude Southern writers certainly. Stark Young was a distant cousin of mine.

Jones: I didn't know that.

Spencer: Well, my grandmother that married the McCain was a Young from Old Middleton. Then there was another branch of that same family that was at Como. They were Youngs. Some of these moved eventually to Oxford. He was brought up in Oxford but the family came from Como.

Jones: Did you know him?

Spencer: Oh, yes. Mr. Stark. Now, he came to make a speech to the Southern Literary Festival at Oxford that first spring I was there, '49, and I never had a lovlier time. My book had just come out and received good notices, *Fire in the Morning*, and both he and John Crowe Ransom had read it and welcomed me. Stark particularly seemed to take a liking to me. We wrote for years. He recommended me for a Guggenheim. When I was in New York he took me to lunch. That's what I mean. If Faulkner had been like that I would have been happy to try to be his friend. But there was just this enclosure—part, I think, of his art. But Stark was very receptive and really kind. Some of the correspondence he wrote me has since been published with his letters. So it was a nice relationship. But I never read Faulkner until I was in graduate school in Nashville. In a modern novel course I read him. The first semester was Modern British Novelists. It was excel-

lent. Then I went on and took Modern American
Novelists and inevitably hit on Faulkner. I immediately
decided that since I was from Mississippi I would write
a paper on one of Faulkner's books, and I wrote the
paper and then discovered how woefully ignorant I was
of what he was doing and the scope of it. Very little
Faulkner criticism had been published at that time. It
was a mystery of how the whole pattern of the county
was fitted together. This was a great discovery, but I
found it very late. Then I began to read everything he
wrote. I know that some of his influence got into my
work because I was from north Mississippi, so that was
all I knew to write about. We were looking at the same
things, like Italians painting madonnas—the same subject occurs over and over and over. I had to find some
independence. But I don't think—do you think my
books are too much like Faulkner's, the early ones?
What do you think?

Jones: No, I don't. That's something I wanted to ask
you about though, that charge. *This Crooked Way*, for
instance, was likened to *Absalom, Absalom!*, and also to
his brother John's *Dollar Cotton*. It seems to me the
similarity ends with *Dollar Cotton* after you state the
basic plot of two poor hill country men coming to the
Delta and striking it rich, Amos Dudley and Otis
Town.

Spencer: But see, I never read *Dollar Cotton*. And I
never thought about *Absalom, Absalom!* because the
scale was so much more modest in that *Absalom* was
pre-Civil War, and there were the magnificent mansion
and millions of slaves and the dynasty thing. This made
it an entirely different scope from what my novel pur-
ported to be, which was a novel of a man with a religious obsession. I don't think Sutpen had a grain of a
religious obsession, do you? He was obsessed, but it
was social. Okay. I never thought of *Absalom, Absalom!*
because the scope was so different, and the time. *Dollar*

Cotton I never read. So I guess the influence that I had to work myself out of was stylistic. I deliberately had to pull back if I found myself writing what sounded like Faulkner. My materials were coming first hand from what I knew from listening and from my own heritage. This is what I was trying to use. When Yankee critics compared me to Faulkner I thought they just didn't know. I suppose some comparison was inevitable.

Jones: Did any of that figure into the sharp stylistic break you came upon in *The Light in the Piazza?* Did you have a harsh reaction to being compared to Faulkner and Miss Welty and others in Mississippi?

Spencer: I think it's inevitable that critics compare. They live on comparison. If you're going to write a critical paper in college you're taught to do that, you know: compare and differentiate and so forth. They always do that. Women writers are compared to other women writers. Southern writers are compared to other Southern writers. Mississippi writers are compared to other Mississippi writers. You know, you can't escape it. You were asking if that made me start to write differently?

Jones: Yes.

Spencer: I think that what made me start to write differently was that I spent five years in Italy before I came to Canada in '58. I'd never written anything about Italy. I'd written *The Voice at the Back Door* when I was in Italy. Then it looked like instead of being away a year I was going to be away five years, and then it looked like I wasn't going to be living in Mississippi, and I thought I could either give up since my subject matter had collapsed, or I could start writing of other atmospheres and sorts of people I'd been encountering for five years, even though that wasn't the South. So I started writing a few stories like that and *The Light in the Piazza* was one of them. I didn't plan it to be a

short novel. I planned it to be about twenty pages long,
and suddenly it took off and became what it is: over
100 pages long. It was a new experience. But I loved
Italy. I could see things happening in Italy the same
way I could see them happening here. But then I
thought it would be exciting to be a sort of roving
spirit in one's work instead of a fixed planet. You
know? And then I started trying other backgrounds.
But the Southern sensibility is something that's sort of
ingrained in me. If I get too far away from that sensibility, I don't think I'll be able to write.

Jones: What about Miss Welty here in Mississippi,
that influence. Did it intimidate you?

Spencer: I often think that Eudora is even more an
individual writer than Faulkner. I think you have to be
Eudora to write one of her sentences. No, I don't think
her work, except for giving me great delight, has had
any effect on my work. Do you?

Jones: No.

Spencer: I can't see it at all. No, I do think I am a
distinctly different writer. I think I read her later. She
was publishing later. I went through the big Faulkner
kick of reading everything he wrote—that ended about
1942 with *Go Down Moses.* I don't think his work since
that date has had the enormous impact to me that the
earlier ones had. Eudora was just beginning publishing
during those years, and I think I read most of the
things as they came out. But I read her as a writer that
was sort of concurrent with me. Faulkner was a great
idol. Her work seemed to me to be forming a little
ahead of my own. I think only in recent years she's
finally gotten the recognition she deserves, don't you?

Jones: Oh, yes.

Spencer: I used to say I liked her work extremely, and
people would say, "Now who is that?" It would be sort
of like that. People that knew anything didn't say that.

No, I wouldn't say she was an influence I had to fight off.

Jones: Who was? Who would you point to as your greatest influence?

Spencer: Writers don't like to admit that they've been influenced by anyone. But I think that when I started writing I'd been impressed by Thomas Hardy, his novels, because I'd been brought up in a farming background with a whole lot of family lore, with Anglo-Saxon people. The way he constructed his books seemed to me to be almost architectural. I think I tried in *Fire in the Morning* to pay attention to the way he constructed his books. I wanted to build something on my own that would be my own. But I guess structurally he would have been an influence. Certainly more than a writer like Virginia Woolf. She has a kind of magic in a way. But her novels are so fluid. A Hardy novel was laid like a structure, and I could see that.

Jones: Anyone else?

Spencer: I liked Conrad a lot; I think Faulkner was influenced a lot by Conrad if you want to talk about influences. That depended a lot on rhetoric. Conrad relied on the power—masculine power, mind you—evocation and descriptive force and great rolling rhetoric. I didn't aspire to that. I thought it was wonderful stuff.

Jones: Let me ask you something about themes. With the Armstrongs in *Fire in the Morning* and the Morgans in *This Crooked Way* there exists something that literary historians these days are pointing to as inspiration for the outpouring of great fiction and fiction writers in the South from '25 to '55. It has been said that one of these great themes was coming to grips with the Southern family romance.

Spencer: The family romance?

Jones: Yes.

Spencer: In connection with Ary Morgan in *This Crooked Way?*

Jones: Yes, that strong attachment to family.

Spencer: Yes, well, some Southern families talk about themselves and each other as though they were the Plantagenets, even though they may be perfectly ordinary middle-class people. You know?

Jones: Yes.

Spencer: I likely satirized the Morgans, I think, but on the whole I thought they were a family of some dignity. They had their little family stories. But the main reason I made them what they were and the way they were was to show up the noncivilized origins of Amos Dudley. The contrast there helped me bring him in sharp focus. That's really a one-man book. It is so dominated by this man. In the end he's not a great person to be central to a civilization the way Sutpen wanted to be. I wasn't intentionally thinking of this at the time, mind you, but just looking back. He had to be shown as the dominant figure in the book, without having very many credentials to make him that way. It was kind of a religious strain, a primitive religious strain in the South that I was interested in showing. In bringing the Morgans into it I could show what he was and what he believed by showing what he wasn't and didn't believe. It's easy to pick up a family like the Morgans in Mississippi. There may be some literally named Morgan, though I did not have anyone in mind. I was thinking of a family over around Greenville or— oh, where else could a family like this exist? Meridian, Columbus, anywhere. I thought there was that family consciousness any number of places.

Jones: Let me ask you a question about *The Voice at the Back Door.* You are dealing with the tricky area of race relations in the South—I believe the book came out in 1956.

Spencer: Yes.

Jones: Knowing as you did the racial situation in the South at that time, was there something in your mind that you were trying to bring across to the reader, a sense of morality in terms of race relations with the example of Duncan Harper?

Spencer: Let's see. How all that came about was that up until the time I wrote that book I had taken the traditional attitudes more than I should, I suppose. I had actually believed what my forebears had told me about the inferiority of the black race. You know, I realized the time of personal examination had come. I wrote the book to explore any number of attitudes toward the changing social climate. I felt things were going to change. I didn't know they were going to change so violently and dramatically. I'd worked on a newspaper in Nashville, and it was a liberal newspaper, the *Nashville Tennessean,* and I had heard a lot of talk about more liberal policies toward the blacks. When I was at Ole Miss there were people who were somewhat tending that way.

Jones: Dr. Silver.

Spencer: Well, okay. Others too. I thought then that there could have been a student at Ole Miss who'd gotten somewhat exposed to this kind of thinking. You know, Duncan Harper was just a fair-minded man who'd been away in the army. Also, he'd known a kind of scope and perspective beyond just the local by having been an All-American football star. This could have given him more of a horizon, a perspective. Then there was that other man in there who was very attractive, but he was sort of a bad boy, and the other one was the good boy. I thought they were both equally attractive.

Jones: Tallant.

Spencer: Jimmy Tallant. He also had been exposed to a wider scope of thinking, and at the end he came out on the liberal side of things. I was trying to explore it

from a local standpoint really, even though they'd had
outside experience to see how things even in small
towns might be in flux. One certain thing was it was
no longer static. There were forces working for change.
I wanted to see one situation in action. But I deliberately planned the book like a melodrama with a sheriff's
race, a possible murder, this and that. There were a lot
of cross currents like that. I got into it and had a really
good time writing it. It came out shortly after a really
dreadful crime in Mississippi that had received national
publicity: the Emmett Till murder, which you won't
remember.

Jones: 1955.

Spencer: Yes. And it coincided with a lot of racial
upheaval all over the country. This gave it a national
popularity, reputation, huge critical notice. That was
just purely and simply coincidence. I hadn't foreseen
any of it. I thought it would be a fairly quiet novel,
quietly received as the other books had been. But it did
awfully well. It was translated into about a dozen languages. It was in several paperbacks. It was chosen for the
Time Incorporated reading program. It was in print for
twenty years, and it's now about to be reissued. So
that's quite a distinguished history for a novel. There
are still some people who like to read it. I hope it's not
too dated. I really felt a certain moral pressure to do
this. It was time for me to write a considerable work
because I had two favorably-reviewed beginning novels,
and I knew I was taking an enormous risk to write
something timely that might seem to be a social tract
or might seem to be polemical. You sacrifice more than
you gain. But I still felt obliged to explore my own
thinking about the racial issue. I couldn't avoid it. So
even though I risked the whole thing being lost by just
being timely. . . timely fiction is awful and you should
never try to write it. It may succeed for a day, you
know, and in ten years it's gone. I just had to take that

chance. I think what's kept the book alive is that some
of the characters in it are very real. I enjoyed writing
about them and their speech and the way they met
different situations, not just racial questions but romantic, family, political. I think that they were true
characters.

Jones: Certainly. And when it came out one of the
critics called it "an almost perfect novel," which is a
nice review.

Spencer: Yes.

Jones: You left in 1953 to go to Rome? You were out of
the state really during all the time of racial tension
during which the state underwent so much change. My
question is, is Mississippi today that different from the
Mississippi that you grew up in and knew before you left
in 1953? Is there a real discernible difference in the social
tone here?

Spencer: Well, I remember the South of my childhood
as being a great deal poorer. You see, the whole landscape has changed. You have all these soil conservation
projects. Talking about the Delta, it's not recognizable
from what I used to know. It's still flat. To me it's
perfectly beautiful down here now, even though there're
many parts that seem to have gone. Like North Street
in Jackson. I had some cousins living on North Street,
the corner of North and George Street, and I asked to
be driven by there to see the old house. There's a Span-
ish-looking bank there now. All of North Street is
gone. It's just that prosperity changes things more than
almost anything else. I think it's a prosperous part of
the world here now. These changes are just inevitable.
No, I don't find much of the atmosphere that I grew up
in. But, still, as long as I know people I knew back
then—they seem pretty much the same with the accent
and the friendliness and all that—so much has not
changed. Don't you find that's true? Have you spent all
your life here?

Jones: Yes.

Spencer: Never been away?

Jones: I've been away a lot. I really don't know. I grew up after the social change, really, so I really don't know much about Mississippi before integration personally. And I don't know first-hand anything about life in rural Mississippi.

Spencer: Yes.

Jones: What about writing about Mississippi today as you do, completely out of memory? Do you come back down to fill your well springs?

Spencer: Well, one would hope to. It's not out of memory though. Let's see. I was in Rome for two years. I spent a year in the States finishing *The Voice at the Back Door,* and I was in Mississippi for about a month that year. Well, this is just personal.

Jones: Good.

Spencer: I had just been going with John, my husband, for a couple of years. We wanted to get back together. I didn't want to marry a foreigner, but the farther away I got from him the more I missed him. He kept writing me. Then I went back to see him and we decided this separation was ridiculous, so we got married. Let's see. That was two years away, but one summer after we were married we spent the summer in Mississippi. I've never been away for very long. Last year you had all that drought and chickens dying and people dying. I wasn't here that year because, again, for personal reasons it didn't seem like the time to come. All during the '70s when my mother and father were in their last years. They wouldn't leave Carrollton to stay with us or anybody else, and I came back quite a bit and stayed sometimes for a month or two at the time. And I would take invitations down here for little readings and things that would just pay my air fare. I read on the Coast and at Natchez and in Jackson and at Mississippi Southern. Anybody who would offer me a

plane ticket I would hop on the plane. So I haven't cut
my ties here. If you mean that you have to write out of
living day to day in a place, then I suppose that would
finish me off, wouldn't it? I wrote a book laid in New
Orleans called *The Snare,* and I was down there a good
bit. So I'm not always in Montreal, or always away.

Jones: When you left the South, did you think that
was the end of your career as a writer?

Spencer: I thought I'd keep on writing, but I didn't
know how successful it would be. See, *The Light in the
Piazza,* for better or worse, really did alter my vision of
what I could do. It expanded me because it was so
fantastically successful. The success was completely unexpected. For some reason everybody seemed to love
that story. It was published in *The New Yorker,* then in
book form. It was taken by a book club, it was made
into a movie. You know, it went through one translation after another. Reviews poured in. I thought,
"Well, maybe I should take a wider scope on things.
Not confine myself to the Mississippi scene." So then I
went on and wrote things that were laid in Rome.
Maybe I made a mistake. Some people seem to think I
did, and lectured me severely.

Jones: Really?

Spencer: Well, they didn't think I should have given
up writing exclusively about the South. I thought I had
proved that this other material was not only available to
me but that I could handle it well. So I went on and
did things that challenged me in a new way instead of
just renewing the tie here. The outer world seemed to
interest me more. I don't know why. It seemed to give
me a bigger horizon.

Jones: Yes, ma'am. Yet you do return to
Mississippi. . .

Spencer: Oh, yes. I never want to break the tie. But I
don't know why I should just concern myself with that.
But a lot of people who are attached to Southern litera-

ture and thought I was writing it well deplored the fact
that I gave up writing it. Well, other things like *No
Place for an Angel, Knights and Dragons,* didn't succeed
as well as I thought they should. Maybe my critics were
right. *The Snare* was laid in New Orleans.
Jones: And you personally don't think it hurt your
fiction leaving the South?
Spencer: Well, it became my fiction, so I don't know
if it hurt or not. You can't say—that's the road not
taken, isn't it?
Jones: Right.
Spencer: You never know. You better watch out.
Every turn you make you can't go back and say, "Well,
I guess I can go back the other way." Then you've
changed.
Jones: What about a story like "Ship Island?" That
came out in, I think, '65. Tell me about that story. It
was one of my favorites.
Spencer: "Ship Island." That was a very significant
story for me. I think it's about my favorite of my
stories. But it started a new theme in my work. I don't
quite know how to put it, but it was the same thing in
The Snare, it's the same thing in some of the stories in
that book *(The Stories of Elizabeth Spencer).* It's that
women feel themselves very often imprisoned by what
people expect of them. You know? Some people mount
rebellion: they are not going to put up with it. This has
come to the surface in many aspects of my later work.
That story was what started it. I just thought it had a
compelling feeling. I felt it was very sensual and very
right, and I liked it a lot. I think I wrote it in '63 and
The New Yorker fooled around. It was long, and *The
New Yorker* has a policy of bringing out seasonal publications. If you write a story that's laid in the summer,
they'll publish it in the summer but they will not
publish it in the fall. So they missed one summer with
it, and they fooled around till the next summer, and I

thought they weren't going to publish it then. It sat around for about eighteen months. I thought they should have come out with it sooner. It needed publishing when it was written. Let's see, then after that was *Knights and Dragons,* and then after that was *No Place for an Angel,* and then after that was the volume *Ship Island,* and then there was *The Snare.*

Jones: But you came across this girl that kind of rebels against this young insurance man just out of the fraternity house and runs off with those two sort of strange men, you came across her spontaneously and thought that that was right? What was her name?

Spencer: Nancy.

Jones: Nancy. You thought hers was a voice that suited you?

Spencer: Well, she didn't come on me as strongly as a voice as a character like Marilee. I think *Ship Island* is a third person story. But for some reason I began to feel an affinity to kind of waif-like women that were free. They have no particular ties, or no ties that are worth holding them, and so they become subject to all kinds of encounters, influences, choices out in the world. You know, they've got to find a foothold, they've got to find something to hold to. This affinity shows up in several stories like that. I think there swings in and out of Nancy's voice that kind of thinking all the way through, and it has the rhythm of the sea all the way through.

Jones: Was "Judith Kane" in that collection?

Spencer: Yes.

Jones: Another one of my favorites. Can you tell me something about that story?

Spencer: A lot of people feel that is a strange story. Some people don't like it. I thought it was very powerful. I thought it was a study of evil.

Jones: Yes. Evil with a beautiful face.

Spencer: Yes. This narcissistic obsession was what was

victimizing the man and the girl that happened into
the house. She perceived that too late to stop—I don't
know if she could have stopped. The girl that tells the
story. The full force of the situation strikes her later on.
Jones: Right. That house I kept picturing right off
campus somewhere in Belhaven.
Spencer: I think I remember setting that in Nashville,
that's where I pictured it taking place. Yes, it had a
thread of fact. Most all my stories, though they develop
into something else, have a thread of something that
suggests them. I remember staying in a rooming house
with three or four of us who were in graduate school.
There was one extraordinarily good-looking girl that
was rather statuesque. I don't think she was in the least
narcissistic, so this isn't trying to portray her as she
was—she was a very nice person—but she had a room
there. She told us one day that she used to walk around
the room naked, and one morning she looked out the
window and there was this boy in the house next door
with his chin on his hand looking down. And it looked
like he'd been doing that every morning since she'd
been there. It gave her the creeps, she said. That was
the end of that when she pulled down the shades. She
was a nice person, and to put her in a neurotic situation
seems unkind. She was very well adjusted. Years later
when I thought of the story I thought of it in connection—I don't know; things scramble themselves—in
connection with some man I'd known, and his determination to get something back whatever the cost. You
know, this kind of thing came together and made a
totally different kind of character out of that incident.
But the setting of that distinctly was Nashville. Don't I
mention that? You thought it was Belhaven?
Jones: I kept picturing a house over near Miss Welty's. I just put you there because I knew you were at
Belhaven when you were the age of the girl in the
story.

Spencer: That's all right.

Jones: What about the story "Sharon?" It walks on shaky ground. Can you tell me something about that story?

Spencer: About the uncle next door that was living with the black maid?

Jones: And had children by her.

Spencer: See, I started this whole series about a girl growing up in Port Gibson, actually.

Jones: Marilee.

Spencer: Marilee. I don't know much about Port Gibson. The country just outside of Port Gibson was nice. It was a partly experienced and partly imagined image. I love south Mississippi, over toward Natchez and Vicksburg, Woodville. It's not the landscape I was brought up in, but for me it seems like a country I know imaginatively very well. I try to think of what's going on there. After I thought of her I put her in a rather plain house, and I thought, "Well, they've been there a long time." It started with a house. There are beautiful houses down that way, and I shouldn't have given her such an ordinary farm house to live in. I thought there must be a family connection. Then out of nowhere Uncle Hernan appeared in the house next door. And then his whole history came to mind. I wanted him to be alone to affect her life without a wife, and yet to be a masculine and virile personality. I realized he would have to have a woman, so the whole story emerged about the wife who died and the furnishings of the house reflecting her taste. Oh, I don't know. It just formed itself. If you put enough chemistry into a story it will make its own element. Do you write?

Jones: No, ma'am. Just interested. But I thought that was a fascinating story. Did you ever get any feedback on that?

Spencer: Yes, a lot of people seemed to like it. I read it once at a writer's workshop or conference in Indiana.

One of the teachers was a rather militant black poet. I was a little nervous about reading it. I don't think she stayed to hear that. But some of the black people who were at the conference came up later and told me they liked it very much. I think that it would seem like a considered portrayal of all that to any black person who wasn't extremely militant. A militant black would have resented the fact that I represented Uncle Hernan in a favorable light at all, I think. Don't you?

Jones: Yes.

Spencer: He would have had to be some awful slob.

Jones: Yes, and maybe they would have resented that she submitted to it.

Spencer: Yes. And that he didn't honor his children, you know. They didn't go by his name, and he didn't send them to college and things like that. I guess that would have entered into their thinking, as of course it would have to.

Jones: Very interesting. Tell me about writing your short stories as compared to writing your novels. You said that *The Light in the Piazza* started off as a twenty-page short story and just grew. Do your novels grow out of your short stories?

Spencer: Well, no. That's about the only one, I think. *Knights and Dragons* did start as a short piece, but there were too many mysterious things in it and I thought I would clarify all that by just writing a little more and a little more, and finally it was what it is. No, generally the longer novels have all started as novels. It was just those short novels that were just sort of extensions of short stories. I do think *Light in the Piazza* is like a novella, you know. It has the balance and proportion of a . . . mini-novel. I generally do undertake to write a novel. Sometimes I'll start those tiny little stories re-published in the collection just on an impulse, just to see how far that will take me. I sometimes think that if you start something like that it may form itself very beautifully, like a little miniature. In six pages you can just see it, you know. It's like a little thing that has just sprung up. I do them in one afternoon. But a longer story that involved character and content—I have one coming out in *The New Yorker* this week. I started it as a story and it developed as a story. Usually those longer ones go through two or three writings. The first time I do them they are twenty-five or thirty pages long, and they almost invariably don't satisfy me. I'll mess around with them for a while, and then I'll put them back, and then two or three months later I'll get it out and see what it really needs. It may not need much rewriting, but it will need touching up. Most of the time they will come about. Aren't you tired of asking me questions?

Jones: Gosh, no. Are you tired?

Spencer: No, no.

Jones: Do you need to go?

Spencer: No.

Jones: I think this is fascinating. Certainly I'm not tired of asking you questions. I'll just ask you a couple more.

Spencer: All right.

Jones: I was reading a review of your book of short stories in the *New York Times Book Review* by Reynolds Price in which he says that you see the Southern bourgeois female as a mirror of the world. Is that fair to you?

Spencer: No, I didn't like that. I was glad that he praised the book, that he came up with favorable things to say about my work. But as an appraisal I get sort of lost in that criticism, because I don't think I'm particularly middle class any more than any other writer from the South. The South had aristocratic pretensions, or cultivated aristocratic traits, but it seems to me that we're all predominantly middle class here. The other thing he seemed to ignore was that many of the longer

stories like "Ship Island" or "I, Maureen" or several of
the others are about women who are at odds with the
middle-class view of life, you know. To them it *isn't* a
sufficient view of the world. It's being tested through
them and found wanting, and they are not going to let
themselves be forced to submit to it. The other thing
he missed is that some of the stories aren't even about a
woman's view. A good many of them are about children. One or two of them have male protagonists.
What can I say? To give that as a generalization on the
stories seems to me to be a bit off-putting for a reader
and not fair to the collection. But I felt he should be
thanked for taking an overall favorable view of my
work. I don't want to criticize Reynolds Price. But that
did kind of rub me the wrong way.

Jones: Do you think you've gotten just criticism over
the years? Do you think that the critics have gotten
what you've put in your books?

Spencer: Well, no. Am I supposed to sit here and say
that I am such a great writer and that they are missing
it? You are putting me in a position of . . .

Jones: No, all I'm asking is if you feel as if you've
gotten your just criticism, that your message has been
received as you intended it to be.

Spencer Well, I think that up through *Light in the
Piazza* I had a good many favorable—I had the favored
regard of a great many people. I think *Knights and
Dragons* was a story that was widely misunderstood, and
possibly shouldn't have been published as a separate
novel. I was very tentative about it. I wanted it in a
collection and the publishers wanted to bring it out
separately. I think it lost me a wider audience and I had
to get that back. I don't think enough attention was
called to the next novel or *The Snare*. How can I say? I
may be wrong. Maybe they don't succeed as well as the
others. But I thought in each case they didn't receive
the notice they should have. How can I tell? Maybe

there were other writers that were more interesting at the time they came out. Critics tend to take the whole spectrum of what's appearing, you know. They look horizontally, whereas a writer is always building out of the past and into the present—not exactly a progress but a development. You know, you don't want to repeat yourself. Unless the critic takes the writer as a special focus of interest and shows how each book has advanced and developed him, then you're not being given the best judgment. But then very few critics have that much time to do that, or want to bring that much time to your work. Faulkner began to receive that kind of criticism only in the last years of his life only because of the accumulated body of the work hadn't been widely understood or favorably received before. He had to educate a whole new line of critics, you see, to come up to where he had already passed.

Jones: Yes, he was out of print until 1947.

Spencer: Not only out of print. Sometime look in *The New Yorker* magazine—maybe you already have—and read the review of *Absalom, Absalom!* that was written I think by Clifton Fadiman when it came out. Have you seen that?

Jones: No.

Spencer: The craziest thing you've ever read in your life. You know, silliest book he ever read, and he made fun of it for four or five pages of *The New Yorker*. And I think that's one of Faulkner's masterpieces.

Jones: You've said that you always think that your next work will be your definitive work, your best.

Spencer: Oh, you always feel that the next thing will be greater than the last one. You want me to talk about the next thing?

Jones: Yes.

Spencer: Well, I don't much want to because I have been fooling around with this novel for a long time. Occasionally it seems to come about me as something

that could be a very strong and wonderful work. I hope
it will finally make it. Sometimes it seems elusive. It's
laid on the Gulf Coast. That's one reason I came down
here, because I needed to get down to where the scene
actually takes place. I can always write much better in
those circumstances. It may turn out to be a short,
minor work instead of a longer thing. I'm just not
quite sure at this point. You go through that in writing
any novel. William Styron said on the Dick Cavett
show that writing a novel is like "trying to crawl from
Vladivostok to Madrid on your knees." I thought that
was good. Did you see that?

Jones: No.

Spencer: It was funny.

Jones: Well, I'll let you go. I appreciate your sitting
and talking with me and being so very nice. It's been
interesting. I'm glad I got to meet you.

Spencer: It's good to meet and talk to an interviewer
who has actually gone and read your work. I've been
interviewed by people who start off by saying, "I've
heard about you and I'd like to read something you've
written." I always want to say, "Well, what's stopping
you?" You've been very good.

Jones: I've enjoyed reading your work. Thanks again.

Photograph by Christine Wilson

Barry Hannah

¿

December 26, 1980

I got the news on Christmas Eve that Barry Hannah was
in town and had agreed to an interview. When I arrived
at his parents' home in Clinton at dusk on the day after
Christmas I found him watching his sons throw the
football in the front yard. He is a thin man with a great
smile, and on the day of our interview wore white
cowboy boots, jeans and a blue, hooded sweatshirt bearing a "Ray" silk-screen design on the breast to advertise
his latest novel. He is also a very funny man, adept at a
variety of accents. I meant to disparage no one when I
gave these idioms the designations that I did in
transcribing the tape. We sat in the living room and
talked for a couple of hours while smells of the supper his
mother was cooking penetrated the cigarette smoke from
time to time. Later I stood around the table with eight
members of the Hannah family and held hands as Barry's
father blessed the fried oysters and ham.

Hannah: Is this like Nixon's? Everytime I tell a lie it
turns on? That was good, you know, it gave us that
much history.

Jones: Right. Let me say this. This is John Jones with the Mississippi Department of Archives and History, about to interview Mr. Barry Hannah. It's the day after Christmas 1980, and we're at Barry Hannah's parents' home in Clinton, Mississippi. With us is the lovely and charming Miss Maribeth Kitchings, Mr. Hannah's niece. Is this house where you grew up, in this home?

Hannah: A good bit of it. There is an erased house on Main Street uptown in the old village part that I lived in until I was around fifteen.

Jones: Were you born here in Clinton?

Hannah: No.

Jones: Tell me something about your early life.

Hannah: Well, there's not much to it. I was born in Meridian in a hospital, but our home really was in Forest, out from Forest in Scott County. Then my folks lived on the Coast a while, lived in Pascagoula. Then, because of my Mama's asthmatic condition, we had to move upstate and my father brought us here to Clinton.

Jones: What did your father do, or does he do?

Hannah: Dad was for twenty-five or more years an insurance agent for New York Life, a very fine salesman. But he's had car dealerships and some real estate, he's been in banking. You know, it's been all business pretty much.

Jones: Yes. You graduated from Clinton High and went straight to M.C.? [Mississippi College]

Hannah: Yes.

Jones: Four years at M.C.?

Hannah: Four wonderful years at M.C., yes.

Jones: Tell me, was there someone here in Clinton who was an early intellectual mentor for you, maybe someone who instilled in you an early love for the language?

Hannah: Yes. There must have been something at home. We were rich in Bible, for one thing. But mentors outside that really encouraged me came about in

third grade. Mrs. Bunyard was a woman of large experience and appreciation, and she used to let me get by
with short stories when others were doing serious work.
That was nice. I also remember a woman who is still
actively mentoring others over at Millsaps: Mrs. Lois
Blackwell taught me what poetry was and introduced
me to drama and music and French and maybe the
world; an amazingly marvelously learned lady who was
very generous to brats like me in the tenth grade. At
Mississippi College I was fortunate enough to have
some instruction in appreciation, especially from a man
who's dead, very regrettably: Joe Edgar Simmons, a
poet of note, a fine poet. I took his classes. Certainly
there were others. Louis Dollarhide was very encourag-
ing, always on my side. There was, when I was at
Mississippi College, a real literary interest, and for
some reason or another, good English instruction. I
profited from the Lipseys there, Mr. Pete Lipsey in
history. He introduced me to history. I don't want to
leave out also a really influential man named Dick Prenshaw, who was my high school band director. When I
went to high school, you either played football or, I
don't know, maybe you were queer.

Jones: Same thing when I went.

Hannah: Yes, we had a marvelous band that won all
the awards and went places. It made you proud of
yourself if you were not being brutalized on the field. I
mean you could hold your head up! As a matter of fact,
the jocks envied us, which was quite a note. So I want
to include Mr. Prenshaw, who's at Mississippi Southern
now.

Jones: Peggy Prenshaw's husband?

Hannah: Her husband, yes.

Jones: Did you play the trumpet?

Hannah: Sure did, yes. All that goes along with being
a musician, John, was very valuable. And travel. I want
to include my parents too. My Dad always took me

along on these trips that he won by being a marvelous salesman, you know, Top Club and President's Club. They'd take me out of school, you know. It was all right. It was kind of loose back then. So I was well travelled when I was twelve years old, you know: Miami, Canada. That's pretty good for a Mississippi boy. And out West. You pick up as much travelling as you do in the classroom, you know that. The same with our band. Our band was cosmopolitan! We read *Downbeat,* you know, and kept up with the world at large. The paper curtain didn't really cocoon us like it did others. We knew there was something outside, and sought it.

Jones: Yes. That Dream of Pines Marching Band in *Geronimo Rex* was fashioned after some of the things you saw touring around with the Clinton High Band?

Hannah: Yes. I saw some good black bands in Mississippi. I don't think anybody's missed them. They take it seriously, a lot of them.

Jones: Yes.

Hannah: I mean *real* men in those things. I mean they trot, man, they're fast! They will blow you away, you know, if you're interested. I saw in Enid, Oklahoma, on one of these band trips you know with Clinton High, and I saw that there were bands, and then there was this other band. It was us and them, I mean. It was like somebody had dropped out from Mars. The categories were just discarded! They were beyond. They were quick, you know: d–d–d, d–d–d, d–d–d, d–d, d–d, d–d–d, d–d–d, and smoke was coming off the field! It was kind of scary! And this was Bossier City, baby, and they were good. You know, a lot of jaws dropped. You know, triple ones in everything. Superior, you know, wow! So maybe a little of them, and the whole mystique, and the absurdity, really, of having that kind of show out of what should be low-rent creeps at some high school—you know, pros at sixteen! You just know somebody's behind it. You just wonder.

Jones: Yes. After you finished M.C. did you go straight on into graduate school?

Hannah: Yes, right into the University of Arkansas.

Jones: Yes. I interviewed Jim Whitehead last month.

Hannah: Yes, I saw him last year.

Jones: Was he an influence on you?

Hannah: Yes. Although Jim didn't teach me in the classroom he taught me a lot outside, especially in the snooker parlor. That's the good thing about graduate school: it loosens up your education, it goes outside the classroom so much. You got something you want to do, and you pick up on things. It's like you're a lint instrument or something. You just hang around and you get an education if you don't watch it. Jim was very good. He took poetry so seriously I said, "My God, it must be worth something." To see some man like that take art seriously will change you. Again, it made me say, "Well, this is worthwhile. This man is passionate about what he does." I kind of was a dabbler, you know the kind on college campuses: they write and the sensitive girls like it. You keep dropping these stories, you know, and they are probably dreadful. But it was on that level that I was writing.

Jones: For the ladies here at M.C.

Hannah: Yes, you know, I had a reputation for stories that nobody could figure out. I never told them I couldn't either. I was a mysterious young man and all that, with a strange crowd. I enjoyed it, enjoyed the hell out of it. What were we talking about?

Jones: Jim Whitehead and graduate school.

Hannah: Yes, he's a good man. I stayed with him, as a matter of fact, in Fayetteville. He's got seven children. They are beautiful and polite. You can tell they're from Mississippi. Their Mama is a gorgeous Delta lady.

Jones: Gen, yes.

Hannah: Yes. It was just a glorious reunion.

Jones: What about the academic training for a writer? Do you believe in the role of academics in the creative process?

Hannah: Yes, finally. I don't teach anymore. I'm glad. I might do a little teaching out at Occidental this spring, but that's just to pay the rent. But after all is said and done, and experiencing a lot of people—you know, I've seen students drop out and say, "This ain't it, school," and it doesn't have to be. There are not many of them who make it, "IT," out on their own, you know?

Jones: Yes.

Hannah: I believe in the theory of dropping out and writing, but I don't see it coming through too much. Some kind of discipline, if it's a good school or a half-ass school, is good. There's something about putting yourself down in school that's instructive, if you let it. One teacher out of twenty is fine, you know?

Jones: Yes.

Hannah: So, yes. And it doesn't hurt to read books, and it doesn't damage you to know history and all you can. Eventually it is going to come forth in your sentences. Even if it's not on that subject, it's going to shine someway. Somebody's going to say, "That man knows what he's talking about," or, "This man is faking it."

Jones: Fabricating his information.

Hannah: Yes.

Jones: Yes. It's been interesting talking to some of the Mississippi writers to see that the ones who teach in college usually say education is important if not vital, and then one like Shelby Foote, you know, who quit undergraduate school, says that really nothing worth anything is coming off college campuses these days, that most every poet you know is stuck off away from life somewhere on a college campus doing nothing besides laying the coeds.

Hannah: I'm with Shelby on that point. But then I've been antipoetry for years; not the art but the sham, and the lack of product from the campus. I have met a number of suicidal, sensitive people who might write three poems a season that nobody in their right mind would publish but get published and are bragged on, by whom? Each other! It's a very incestuous profession, and very unmanly in most cases. Ideally it should be very brave because you get nothing for it, and that's true. There's something about a mute and inglorious Milton, you know, like Gray said. That's a wonderful idea, but the ones I know are not mute and inglorious, and they deserve to be inglorious—with some wonderful exceptions. On the other hand, what Shelby said, who's a marvelous writer—see, you get it different ways and you have different attitudes. How old is Shelby?
Jones: Sixty-four.
Hannah: Yes. Well, he has done his stroke and probably appreciates sweat and toil. He probably hasn't seen a lot of school fiction. When I was at Alabama I certainly saw some young, worthwhile stuff in my fiction classes. I don't say that just because I was the boss. There was some very fine stuff coming out of there. So I'd be more positive about it than Shelby.
Jones: Right. It's hard to generalize.
Hannah: Yes.
Jones: Was your early writing poetry? Did you start off with the intention of becoming a poet, or was prose always what you were interested in?
Hannah: I guess I'm too much of an exhibitionist to really believe in poetry. I never was satisfied with the small tome read by your friends. At an early age it looked like that kind of business to me. I think when I found the short story I knew it was really my thing. Although I'm not always the foremost plotter in America, I do like the story, the yarn, the tale. I split it up. Lately I've been using short sentences. But there's still something going on! *Ray* is awfully short. If

I accomplished what I wanted to in there—see, I threw away about 400 pages from that book. It itself has been called poetic. Now I did not say that, okay? This is not Barry Hannah bragging on himself.

Jones: Yes. I know, I've read some of the reviews.

Hannah: Yes. You tend to like things like, some guy in *Newsweek* said: "Although the man is confused and you might expect confusion, it is like holding up a finely chiseled gem." I went, "I love it!" I think I'll send him a thank you note. That's what I was shooting for, you know?

Jones: Yes.

Hannah: It is not a random book. Ray is a doctor, and he's trying to be a poet for one thing, and he ain't too hot.

Jones: Not much compared to Mr. Hooch.

Hannah: Mr. Hooch lays him down. But he is sparse. The doctoring business is short and sweet. You don't want a sonnet out of someone who's treating you. I thought it fit the man. I think that's what poetry does often with the speaker, you know? The voice is the man. If I was writing about a sensitive aunt in Itta Bena I'd be completely different. There'd be more lyricism and a gathering of history. Ray really don't give a damn for history.

Jones: You don't?

Hannah: Ray doesn't.

Jones: What about the references to Jeb Stuart and the Confederate cavalry?

Hannah: All right, I just contradicted myself. He cares for specific battle history. He says, "Ah, I'm caught in two centuries," but look what he goes to: the charge. He's always right in the middle of the charge or right before the battle, or he goes to Vietnam right before they're blowing everything apart. He does not go back to the stately mansions of old, or any era. There has been one particularly interesting review by some

low-level creature. It was the only negative one I got.
But he said something that does not apply to *Ray*. I took
a false beating on that for a lot of other Southern
writers. He said, "These people seem to be in a deliber-
ate conspiracy to misunderstand their own past." That
was by Arnold Klein, or something. Well, you know,
Mr. Klein is wrong! Ray understands his past pretty
good. Southerners do! They are the only ones who care
about it! You know? You get to California and a guy
doesn't even know where his grandfather is! For one
thing the guy has been married twelve times, you
know, and he's probably been through Esalen, and they
lose each other out there. I'm a freak, you know. "You
going back to Mississippi to visit your people? What a
sensitive man!" My God, you know. I was on that
jumbo jet and it was full of Mississippi folks. Sure we
go back to see our people. I don't like historical slobs,
you know, who just live in it forever. You don't want
to go to their party either, you know. Ray doesn't
misunderstand his own history. As a matter of fact he
was in a big part of Vietnam. You tend to understand
things you've been through and survived.
Jones: Yes. Let me ask you this question which will
probably seem pretty stupid, but has something to do
with Southerners and their history. I read a book recently called *Southern Renaissance.*
Hannah: Oh, another one?
Jones: Another one.
Hannah: I haven't heard about this one.
Jones: It says that what produced so much fine Southern fiction in the '25 to '55 period was that the writers
were trying to lay history to rest, trying to come to
terms with the family romance. Do you believe that?
Hannah: No. Lay history to rest? How do you do
that?
Jones: Write it down to get it off your mind, I guess.
Hannah: No. Who wrote that?

Jones: Richard King.

Hannah: He doesn't know what he's talking about, unless you've misquoted him. It sounds to me like an awfully stupid thing to say.

Jones: That's the sense I got from the book: to come to grips with the family romance . . .

Hannah: So that you can get along and be a real estate person now? "Let's get this McDonald's show on the road," or what?

Jones: Right. He's talking specifically about the writers from '25 to '55, Faulkner to Miss Welty.

Hannah: Miss Welty tries to lay history to rest?

Jones: That's what he says inspires her fiction. You know the Southerner's burden of history argument.

Hannah: Oh, like in *Absalom, Absalom!* where the guy is eaten up by his past, he can't believe it, can't comprehend it and finally blows his head off. Yes, all right. A lot of Southern fiction is full of that. But if you mean just to write it out so you can forget it, I don't think so.

Jones: I'm sure I'm simplifying it.

Hannah: Yes. Well, my fiction is always full of pain. I think a lot of writing is full of pain. You get hurt and you tend to remember, if you're human. I don't deliberately go around inventing painful situations so that I may live to tell the story, like poets do often. I don't think about it too much. But it comes along, and telling it does—I'll tell you, it doesn't really decrease the sorrow for me, but at least it puts it out there for you. Maybe there is some kind of anesthetic benefit finally. But pain tends to hurt. I don't know if you can get it out by literature. Maybe some.

Jones: Yes. What about that Mississippi literary tradition, does that mean anything to you?

Hannah: It didn't used to. I used to really avoid it. As a matter of fact, I went through a really snotty period when I didn't really like to be known as a Mississippi

writer. I still don't like to be known as specifically
Southern because that will get you in all kinds of diseased catagories, and people will ignore your book that
shouldn't. But who's Southern? Donald Barthelme is
Southern. It does not have to be the slammed screen
door and the crazy aunt all the time, you know? Well,
Barthelme is awfully good, and he is awfully un-South-
ern in that way. I'm Southern and I'm proud of it. If
you mean a heritage from Faulkner to Miss Welty to
Tennessee Williams to Elvis Presley to B. B. King,
then my God, yes, I am proud to share it. You better
believe it. But I don't like Faulkner for the old mansions and the decaying families, the sickness, patholog-
ical history. I don't like Faulkner for that. There's just
so much else to like in him. He probably couldn't have
got it if he'd been in Ohio. Sherwood Anderson was
from Ohio and he taught Faulkner all that cup of tea.
But if you mean those people, I am more than proud to
be in their party, yes.

Jones: But did they influence your writing?

Hannah: Not consciously. But if you read something
like "Powerhouse" by Miss Welty and you were a young
musician something's got to rub off. That's a powerful
piece of jazz work. It's amazing—and I hope that
women won't feel bad about this, Maribeth; my niece
I'm talking to—and this is not an antiwoman statement, but I am shocked that a woman knew that much
about a travelling musician. Just shocked! Usually a
woman in that place would be a teenage groupie who
does not get any of the point, you know, who tries to
grab at his clothes for a one-nighter at best. She could
not understand—what's his name? "Powerhouse."

Jones: I can't remember. [The musician's name in the
story is Powerhouse.]

Hannah: That's a goody. I'm sure Miss Welty, and I
read her very thoroughly, and Faulkner and the short
story had a lot to do with the way I shape them. You

can't get away from that, you know, even if you wanted
to. But on the other hand, I think I've done some
things that have nothing at all to do with that mode.
Jones: Oh God, yes.
Hannah: And it should not be copied after all, you
know; it's theirs.
Jones: Those that try it and do it poorly really stink.
Hannah: Yes.
Jones: But was that old Southern Gothic tradition
something that you wanted to work against?
Hannah: Yes. I use it. I think it's a wonderful background for all kinds of farce. You know in *Geronimo Rex*
that spooky old house that Whitfield Peter lives in is a
fraud, a complete phony. Things happened in there
that just don't get it on in real life. You know he's got
all the old vines everywhere, and you can just see all the
Hollywood guys come in, (in the nasal tone of a Hollywood director) "All right, let's get the mansion on the
road. All right, get the creepy uncle. Where do you
want the creepy uncle?" I have a mental picture of
somewhere in Madison County, wasn't it?
Jones: Yes.
Hannah: But it was just a set that I cranked up. (In
the same tone) "Okay, you want to get the loony niece
out now? All right, shoot! No! No!" I mean can't you
see how creepy that set is, I mean this young college
boy out there sneaking around in the bushes?
Jones: With a gun.
Hannah: With a gun. Blowing up the guy's Chrysler
or whatever he did.
Jones: He and Silas were hiding near the porch and
hear him talking.
Hannah: Yes, and they discover him there. It's been a
while. I don't read my own marvelous literature all that
much. But, yes, it is so obviously a set, like on "Saturday Night Live." I had fun with it. Well, that's what I
think of, uh . . .

Jones: Your Southern heritage.

Hannah: My Southern heritage, yes. I just wrote a piece for *Esquire* about Southern heritage. There's part of Tuscaloosa that you can have. See, I've owned these homes, that's one of the things, and I never took them that seriously. But people do fall in love with wallpaper. White women will marry stately mansions of old and become as mossy as what grows on it. That's what I said. You know, Tuscaloosa is full of those big things like on North State. But you can have that. That's not what I write about. The people who come to my party, my associates, were always a little bit too un-nice for those folks. They might be invited as freaks, interesting freaks, but you wouldn't want them staying overnight. I like generally the kind of people that blow the mind of the middle class. And the middle class, and their dead lives, infest those things all over the South, and I think it's as big a shame as McDonald's. The big dream is to get upper-middle class and purchase one of those big houses.

Jones: Right. Get your house in *Southern Living.*

Hannah: Right. By the time you get your photograph in there—and this is another terribly categorizing statement—but you can pretty much figure the people are dead. It's too late. They are awful people! Do you ever go to any of those houses?

Jones: More than I want to admit.

Hannah: I mean the people who are supposed to be the repositories of culture, if they're not Snopeses, they are—I mean, they didn't make their money in honest ways usually, or dignified ways.

Jones: They didn't have the plantation.

Hannah: No. They're dentists, you know. Or even Northern. They came down here to get 'em a mansion, baby. Okay, enough sociology.

Jones: No. You do use the Southern capacity for violence, you know, in your work.

Hannah: I don't believe we've cornered the market on violence. There're more murders in L.A. now than the traffic toll. That's not Southern. Southerners write about it, and make it long stories. But yes, there's a lot of violence in my work. Some of it's funny, and some of it is meant. But I don't think I'm coming out the bloodied survivor of a violent tradition.

Jones: I was talking about that twisted, eccentric sort of Whitfield Peter violence that does so much damage in the name of being just and standing up for what you believe in.

Hannah: Yes. Maybe that's dead. Maybe these old creeps from the Klan—even the Klan wears ties now. You noticed that?

Jones: Yes.

Hannah: That new dude over there who claims that his is the real Klan; we thought it was the ones who blew away Viola Liuzzo. Not so, apparently. I'm writing a screenplay right now: *The Big Jim Folsom Story.* You know, decent people in the South have long been against the Klan, they always knew they were poor white trash, most of them. That's what you mean, the Whitfield Peter sort?

Jones: Right.

Hannah: And the letter to the editor and all that. Well, everybody knows it happened. There's something very true in that book that came very close to my father. There was that girl, the girl who went to M.C., she was a nightrider and she tried to bomb a Jewish man's house, and the Meridian police and the F.B.I. teamed up and blew them away. I think it was the first time local police or state police worked against civil rights violators, the Klan. You were too young to remember that.

Jones: I remember my mother telling me the whole story. It was she and her boyfriend. I can't remember the specifics.

Hannah: It was all nasty.

Jones: And in the book Catherine and her lover are killed the same way.

Hannah: Yes. That really happened, and it was nasty, awful. But it might have been a significant turning around point when they found out the cops would shoot you if you tried to bomb people at night.

Jones: Do you feel like Whitfield Peter is exaggerated?

Hannah: I've seen letters to the editor that were just about there. But, of course he's exaggerated some. He's a kind of catch-all for a number of diseased, vicious types that I saw. Maybe they were more prevalent—I'm thirteen years older than you are—maybe they were more prevalent when I was reading the papers. Now they hide more or are just not listened to.

Jones: Must have been an interesting time to be growing up, in the early sixties in Mississippi.

Hannah: Yes. You could get a pistol pulled on you for wearing tennis shoes at one point. If you went to the wrong roadside restaurant tennis shoes meant "hippies," "Freedom Riders." I have trembled coming back to my own state because my hair was a little long. I'm not trying to put on a hero act.

Jones: No, this is all true to what I've learned.

Hannah: Yes. You've probably been in places yourself that you were glad to get out of.

Jones: Right.

Hannah: Yes?

Jones: Certainly.

Hannah: I once forgot it was Sunday when I was coming back and I mentioned something to a clerk or something, and he looked at me pretty dangerously: "Don't forget it's Sunday, my lad." I asked for something you couldn't get on Sunday. He thought that was strange, man, and went out and looked at my car tag.

Jones: Well, did the civil rights movement really change that Mississippi you knew when you were growing up?

Hannah: Obviously it did. Over at E.T.V. you have

blacks working cameras, do you not? I think blacks have quite a bit to do with the operation of cultural Jackson. Do they not?

Jones: Yes.

Hannah: You didn't have that when I was around here. You know, we're talking about things that I cannot be a hero about. I was kind of a coward. I was a little afraid. I was not a civil rights marcher, I was not a Freedom Rider. I was the kind of liberal that is worthless. You admire them a year after, you know?

Jones: Yes.

Hannah: But I ain't going to anybody's jail! So don't give me credit for doing what those young folks did.

Jones: Right. I'm not trying to.

Hannah: I write about it, like writers are good at, from a distance. It's the same thing about Vietnam. My best buddy in Los Angeles flew jets over there. So looking back, it didn't make a whole hell of a lot of difference about my getting up at Clemson and reading antiwar poetry when you look at it. Maybe it did in a way. But I think maybe it was better for Quisenberry to be over there doing something he half believed in, and risking his bottom; although Quisenberry knows right now that it was an ugly, evil war, a useless war. It didn't have to be. Of course I am against Vietnam still. But I see that I was no hero during that era, you know?

Jones: Yes.

Hannah: It's easy to be a hero as a writer anyway. You can have all kinds of emotions and not risk anything, take all kinds of stands. For one thing, I was a little disappointed that no ugly notes came about *Geronimo Rex*. I kind of wanted to stir up something. Not one person sent me a threat. That could have something to do with the fact that people don't read you until you are dead. They love you when you're dead. (Bumpkin accent) "Oh, yeah, that'uz Bill and Elizabeth's boy, wudnit?" And then, you know, the rush! Best thing I could do is keel over. "A place in literature. A Southern tradition." Yes? But I want to say I love the South too. After all the fun is over I love the South. I love the women here. I was at Saturday's the other night, and— you know, you see plenty of beauty in Los Angeles working on the set of *Looker,* which is a Michael Crichton film full of beautiful women. But then there are other beautiful women of a type in Jackson and thereabouts that will just knock your eyes out, but there's something deep. They are gorgeous but there's something ineluctable, how about that?

Jones: That's good.

Hannah: Yes. You know. I think my nieces are that way.

Jones: Absolutely.

Hannah: They can talk, have you noticed that? They can talk, they have some ideas and a sense of humor, besides nice hair and all.

Jones: Right.

Hannah: So, yes, I'm just as chauvinistic about Southern women as anybody. And Southern men too. I think you're a credit, you know. I can tell that you have thought and might have read a book.

Jones: I think you would be surprised how common I am. A lot of my friends have read your stuff along with me and are big fans of yours too.

Hannah: Thank you, thank you. I like it.

Jones: I am interested in the way you use history in all of your works: the civil rights movement in *Geronimo Rex,* the Civil War in many cases, and Vietnam certainly in "Midnight and I'm Not Famous Yet," and *Ray.* Was it something you learned in school? Why is it important to you when you sit down to write?

Hannah: I think the history, John, that has made the difference to me is what I pretty much got on my own. Growing up here, you can almost feel Vicksburg if you're alive. Going over there was a real frequent thing.

You grow up in that park with those gloomy old busts
and those cannons. It's easy to be full of history. You
don't have to be that bright, you know? It's kind of
your heritage if you are around Jackson and Vicksburg.
You know things just by growing up, like Jackson was
Chimneyville, I guess. You know, y'all work at the Old
Capitol; it's just there, baby! It's there! You walk by it
and you eat near it. So you don't have to go to the
library and read about it. And of course I'm very much
into the Vietnam War. I had my best friend over there
fighting in it.

Jones: You never went to write an article or anything?

Hannah: No.

Jones: Your best friend was there?

Hannah: Yes. I say best friend, but I had some wonderful best friends in Jackson too: Joe Brown, who's
Bobby Dove Fleece in the book.

Jones: Is he?

Hannah: Yes. I'm going to see him tomorrow. They
all survived. Nobody's dead. Wyatt Newman lives in
town still. Horace Newcomb teaches at the University
of Texas. We were very close Bohemians of our time,
un-Mississippi College-like folk. Some others. I say
best. Right now John Quisenberry and I are about as
thick as you can get in California. He's a lawyer, just
like Quisenberry in *Ray*. I'm riding his motorcycle to
work. You can just feel Vietnam under you. It came
from Vietnam, a Triumph. I'm going to fly in a Phan-
tom with John. He's a lieutenant commander in the
Navy Reserve now. I still enjoy my friends. You know
how you lose friends from high school?

Jones: Yes.

Hannah: My friends are very much alive and we're still
close. You don't forget. Is that Southern, you don't
forget?

Jones: I don't know if it's Southern. It's certainly true.

Hannah: Yes. So, but the history that's touched me is

nonacademic. It's pretty vivid to me. It comes with
your birth or your times. For instance, I'm not interested in the plantations that much. My mother's a
Delta lady. She came from—her father was a plantation
manager. She's from up around Greenville, Leland, and
has that beautiful thing behind her, which I'm sure I
shared in when I grew up. She married to a landed
gentry, a mid-states person with his good-looking con-
vertible. You forget that parents are people too. That's
something I found out after I was thirty. Mom was very
good-looking. I always knew she was attractive, but she
was a looker, and Dad was laying for her there. See, I'm
talking history now, it's very close to me. You find out
things, John, when you grow older. These things
become meaningful. But not the textbook kind, no. It
just never grabbed me.

Jones: What about a story like "Midnight and I'm Not
Famous Yet," did that come from an anecdote that your
friend told you about the war?

Hannah: No, I made it up, the entire thing. But
when you say, "I made it up," you don't take credit for
everything. The war was there, and your friends were
there. Just little things. There happened to be a guy
that I sort of knew in my high school who was a tank
captain, and I read a little piece about him being engaged in some action sort of like that, a holding action
against a huge army of NVA coming down. You hear
things like that and your mind works and says, "What
if?" and finally you've written a story if you don't watch
it.

Jones: And you read enough to know about phosphor-
ous guns and such.

Hannah: Yes, well, I invented that, but it had to have
been there. They had all sorts of stuff like that eventually. But it's easy history. Maybe Maribeth can recall—
are y'all about the same age?

Kitchings: Yes, close.

Hannah: You woke up every day with that war on your TV, you know. You were watching "The Three Stooges" or whatever, and the next thing on was bloody corpses and body counts. Do you remember the copters always?

Jones: Yes.

Hannah: There was history right in your living room again. You don't have to go out and read it. Any man can write about Vietnam and be believed almost, if he was there. However, not many did that were actually there.

Jones: Perhaps not many can. I was reading an article in *Harper's* about our moral responsibility for Vietnam, and in there a veteran writes a short piece about the war and explains how it is the first and last thing he will ever write about his experiences over there.

Hannah: Yes. Quisenberry's the same way. He's got some notes and has tried to get something together, but can't. See, Quisenberry and I have a mutual admiration society for different reasons. He admires me for writing about the things he went through, being able to, and I admire him for going through them. It's a mutual respect. Maybe that's why we're such good friends. John took me up to Malibu—notice I'm dropping some names in here to make my past interesting— but we had a good trip up to Malibu a couple or three weeks ago. I said, "John, you don't resent the fact that I'm kind of borrowing glory from you with this stuff, do you?" He said, "Not at all. I am just delighted somebody can write it." You know? So it's not like I was showing off like I was an ex-jet pilot, you know. I hate authors—you ever seen these phonies who stand in front of a lion somebody else shot? I think Michener's good on that. You know, really bathe in the culture, at least in time to get that picture taken.

Jones: Right. Hemingway and bullfighting.

Hannah: Yes. Yes, I think Michener is about as sin-

cere as, oh, let's say, Nixon. How can you crank out
that much literature about different places and be sincere, you know? I just wonder. If he is sincere, forgive
me, Mr. Michener. No, I don't believe in a roaming
sincerity like that. Suddenly he's interested in
Chesapeake, ah ha! 2000 pages worth, you know.
That's more like a factory, isn't it?

Jones: That's it.

Hannah: Yes.

Jones: Anything else?

Hannah: That's it. My family has a great deal to do
with my work. I think you can see that. Maribeth and
Hannah and Taylor and Ken and my brothers and sisters; it's not one of these soupy old families. I enjoy my
people, you know, I just love being around them. You
know?

Jones: Yes.

Hannah: Yes. I adore them. They always make me feel
good. We're very strong on letters and moral support,
and we're very loyal. They have a great deal to do with
the positive emotions in my book.

Jones: Maybe that's particularly Southern, to have that
close an extended family.

Hannah: Yes, right. A lot of Californians—and I
don't want to keep nailing Californians because there's
some good, awfully wonderful people there that I work
with, but some of them are not, or they just can't help
it. A lot of them have to go through Esalen or something to feel, you know? Bless their hearts, they think
they are marvelously sensitive and all that for doing
things that you just ordinarily do and don't give a
second thought to. They go through Esalen and maybe
someday some man will hit a woman in the mouth and
she will know that it hurts, and that will complete
their therapy. You know the type?

Jones: Yes.

Hannah: The book readers about "How to Feel,"

"How to Make Love." You know, (In bumpkin accent)
"See here, Marge." My God! "How to Eat."
Jones: "Looking Out For Number One."
Hannah: Oh, yes, those are marvies, aren't they?
Ninety-five cents worth of instant something. "Open
Marriage", that's a good one. They're creeps mainly,
who're frantically sucking around other creeps to find
out what it is, baby, where is it?
Jones: Right. On the whole—let me change directions
again—do you feel like you've gotten a fair shake from
the critics?
Hannah: Yes, except for *Nightwatchmen*. A lot of people liked that book, and I liked it. It was kind of
confusing. America really neglected that by the
thousands. I think it's a decent book.
Jones: I do too.
Hannah: Thank you. It was written quickly, but I
thought I had some interesting things to say in there,
some interesting people.
Jones: I was surprised to see how it was drubbed by
the critics.
Hannah: Yes, it took a round beating. I was attacked
personally for ever even thinking of it. I was attacked
for hastily scraping something together, but it was not
hastily scraped together.
Jones: Mostly imagination?
Hannah: Yes, well, I had a lot of natural background
with Camille, and people I met in graduate school. The
tapes, you know, that was my idea. I like the guy I
invented, old Thorpe Trove, you know—kind of half-
gay or what. He don't know, he can't find it. He's
trying to find his sexuality and himself and love and
place. My God, he's just like a thirty-year-old baby,
you know, and he finds himself in the middle of these
murders and the storm. I also like the old guy he
meets: Howard Hunter, who I modeled after a real guy
up at Clemson. He was one of those delightful older

guys you meet, you know, who haven't lost it. I like
people like that. Survivors. So, you know, it hurt. I got
a good sale out of it, but that doesn't compensate. All
right. My word, there's so much to be thankful for.
Ray is the first commercial success I've had. It's in the
third printing now, you know.

Jones: Been out how long?

Hannah: Since October. A couple of months. I think
it was around 15,000, which is good for me. If that's
not good for somebody else it's wonderful for me, for
this boy. Penguin just bought the paperback, and that's
a good house. Don't get the idea that writers ignore
these things. Unless they got money from their Dad-
dies, or just don't care, and there are a few like that—
but I care. It pays the rent.

Jones: Yes, now that you're not teaching anymore.

Hannah: Yes, it's rather crucial. Some more blue
jeans. That's one thing good about California, and I
guess it's in Mississippi now too, but people are going
around rather comfortable, people in responsible places.
You know, a doctor does not have to be a pale idiot in a
three-piece. He might have longish hair, but that's all
right, you know: Fix me. I like that. You know, it's
new blood.

Jones: Well, in *Nightwatchmen* you kind of stick it to
the academic world; maybe the critics, most of whom
are involved in academia, didn't like anybody running
down their province.

Hannah: Yes, you do get that. A lot of the book
critics are academics, a lot of them, maybe most. You
know, they hold down a position at Yale or Mississippi
Southern. Yes, you know, you're insulting their realm.
I think that war is over. You know the universities are
full of creeps, and that you have to hunt hard to find a
good one. Do I have to state that case? It's kind of
beating a dead horse isn't it?

Jones: It is.

Hannah: Don't you wonder what some of them think, what they feel? "Do you feel this, all this? Can you read those notes year after year, buddy? What do you go home and do? Do you drink water like us?" But as an object of satire that war is over, isn't it? They were all blown out of the water by the young Turks, I believe. They have been repeatedly. People that do wear open shirts know their stuff better than the old dons, you know?

Jones: Yes.

Hannah: Uh oh. You know, the exceptions again are marvelous. One of my good friends—you notice everybody likes to line themselves up with the "real," that's us?—but there's a good friend of mine over at Alabama who's been loyal and faithful and all the things you'd want out of a buddy: a medievalist, an expert; also big on rock and roll, plays in the band with us. You don't have to despise Jimi Hendrix if you know Chaucer, you know? You don't have to take that route in class: (English accent) "Oh, the moderns," you know? Life does go on. Who knows? Hendrix: Chaucer might have dug him a great deal. That's the ultimate irony, that the people they teach would have spat on their lecture notes. You've got these pale people presenting these vivid persons of history who lived lives and loved and fought and gritted. You know, Shakespeare could not have been just your lilac poet. He could not! And, yet, who teaches him usually? The people who go to the Shakespeare Festivals are the people who would've been absolutely ruined by his attacks, you know. They adore him. (English accent) "Oh, isn't he lifelike." He would've just been absolutely gassed by the fact that they load up these 747s and go to England and cry up on Avon—the very creeps that he impugned! Not everybody. There are some healthy, red-blooded people who like Shakespeare, like me. You notice I'm always in the right crowd, Maribeth? You know, "US."

Jones: Is that part of the reason you would take the Confederate tradition of gallantry and all in a story like "Knowing He Was Not My Kind Yet I Followed," and make the main character, a cavalryman with Stuart, gay? Were you kind of thumbing your nose at the traditional methods of teaching history?

Hannah: No, I was not really, John. I sympathize with the gay cavalryman. It must have been a hard thing to be. He's trying to make the move on Jeb, and Jeb is just not interested.

Jones: "May I kiss you, General?"

Hannah: Right. (In gay accent) He's got his glass shop in Biloxi, you know, and, ah, well . . . but Jeb is tolerant. He has a speech about it: "God made you?" One thing about homosexuality: I have never been harmed by a homosexual in my life. In fact, I have been cheered and supported by the homosexual crowd when nice people have fled or ignored. You will find someone who's gay but happens to be an intelligent reader, and takes the art seriously, you know? I have done nothing but profit from that side of humanity. Actually, the gay cavalryman I treat sympathetically.

Jones: Yes, you do. I want to ask you this before we finish—I know your family is getting here.

Hannah: That's all right. It's like I hired them, you know: "Well, here we are."

Jones: Right. Tell me about your concept of lewdness in your work, the way you use sex and rudeness. Is that what's true to you?

Hannah: Yes. Absolutely. I still seem to have managed to come through to those I think are my best readers. They do know it's not pornographic. Pornography is contrived to elicit masturbation mainly. I don't think my work is like that. Ray enjoys sex very much, he celebrates it. I think there's a very solid tradition there, if there's got to be one, in Walt Whitman. It's a part of life, and if you don't want to look at it you're a liar. And you might be embarrassed if it's on the page,

but, my God, it's there, and if you deny it you're
cheating yourself. Maybe it makes people uncomfortable. Some sex in the movies makes me uncomfortable.
It's bad. But if I went into what is dirty and what is
nice it would be awfully complex and very personal.
I'm certain there are people who're blown away by sex
in my work, but the people who write me letters are
not at all, you know? And they are not sexual monsters,
you know?

Jones: Yes.

Hannah: I'm talking about women from Jackson, as
well as men who're not part of the rowdy, risqué crowd.
So that comforts me.

Jones: I think you are right. Did you read Walker
Percy's *The Last Gentleman?*

Hannah: I didn't read all that book, and I'm sorry,
because I like him very much.

Jones: Yes. One of his characters in there is obsessed
with lewdness, sex, pornography, because he says it's
one of the only pure things left in life.

Hannah: Yes, well, we didn't make us, you know
that? We didn't make us. I'm not preaching at you at
all, John. I don't have any preachy messages, by the
way. I like the title of the review I got on *Ray,* and I'm
glad Walker Percy goes along with that: "Rudeness Is
Our Only Hope."

Jones: Our only hope.

Hannah: Right. Of course, I don't want to be rude,
but it beats the hell out of hypocrisy, you know?

Jones: Yes.

Hannah: And the righteous cheats of the world, of
which I've experienced many. It just beats the hell out
of that. I'm not advertising rudeness. Ray is direct, but
who does he hurt finally?

Jones: He hurts his wife.

Hannah: Yes.

Jones: He won't quit drinking.

Hannah: Yes, but that's not rude, that's diseased.
Jones: But you said who does he hurt finally.
Hannah: Not by his rudeness though, not by . . .
okay, you might quibble with that. I don't drink any
more by the way. All of *Ray* is not autobiographical.
There are drunks and then there are drunks. I've seen
some people get away with some monster lies with the
blanket excuse that others drank. I've seen it happen. I
was in the drinking crowd long enough to know that
there are some good and solid people in there. I've
never repudiated that. It's just that I can't handle it
anymore myself. But I do not want to take away the joy
that it gives some who can control it, you know? So,
guilty, you know. Ray is guilty, and has lost a great
deal, and blown away, regrettably, things . . . well,
that's a part of it, being able to see things, too. Usually
a drunk, when he gets well, knows his sins, and has
been through the hell of reliving them. It's like going
to prison, boy. He's at least in that position. And you'll
never find him to be a hypocrite. You know, he does
not forget his own errors. So, but it's better not to be
drunk, isn't it? It is better not to be a drunk, you
know? It would've been better to be a preacher and to
have done it all clean. But, maybe it's because so many
writers drink or something, but they do have a compas-
sion that one who's sinned has. Right?
Jones: Yes, tolerance.
Hannah: Yes. You can push that to a silly degree.
You can get some drunks who'll say, (in drunken slur)
"Well, my God, Hitler didn't drink; let's drink up and
not be Hitler." That's baloney, foolishness! I've heard
that. (Same tone) "Churchill put down a bottle a day
boys, here, have one." That's foolishness. But, drunks,
especially ex-drunks, are generally honest, you know?
They see both sides. Sometimes they cannot quite see
the horror they cause. It's hard for you to be the enemy.
Jones: Ray couldn't see it?

Hannah: Not all of it; never will. After all, you're maiming your instrument of perception there. There's some guy in Jackson getting drunk tonight, and very righteously blowing away somebody, you know, or hurting some girl, or beating a child. And it's going to be a while in the drunk tank before he realizes he is a monster. When he gets arrested he's righteous as hell. You know Ray despises the alcoholic abuser of women and children, you know?

Jones: Yes, but he despises the preacher more. What does he say about the preacher?

Hannah: That book is so short that it's the only one I was able to memorize. No, not really. He says that there are certain perversities like Maynard Castro who know that there are beauties in the world that they can never possess, and so they destroy them. That doesn't mean that you should read *Ray* and say about all preachers, "Nah." This is Ray talking!

Jones: Yes.

Hannah: There are some straight, wonderful guys in the ministry, who love beauty and enjoy others' happiness. But Ray makes all these pronunciamientos from his vantage. You especially know the guy is hurt because his lady has been blown off. Yes?

Jones: Yes.

Hannah: You'd probably be a little sour on preachers at that point too, wouldn't you? He wanted her to sing at Youth Impact and went and killed her before she even got there.

Jones: So pretty he couldn't stand it.

Hannah: Yes. You've seen those who despise people who are pretty, haven't you? You can see them on TV. You figure Lennon, you know? I heard an ex-drunk talk about Lennon, of all people, the other night in California. (In a pompous tone) "Well, if a man messes around with dope and that crowd, influences millions of children, he just bought what he got." This was from a

recovering alcoholic that has brought some woe. I said,
"You know, just because you're a drunk, boy, you want
somebody to blow you away now? Punch your ticket?"
"Well, I wasn't in the public eye." "Well, you were a
Los Angeles policeman, and that's kind of public." It's
hard not to be in the public eye if you really want to
tighten it down, isn't it? And say, "Yeah, let's kill
Lennon. He once used LSD." He also happens to be a
marvelous writer. He hasn't done anything for the last
five years except stay around the house.
Jones: A househusband, yes.
Hannah: Househusband. Some creep will find you
though, you know. "I'm not Lennon so let's bury him."
Have you read much, either of you, about the nature of
the guy?
Jones: Have you seen *Time* this week? Have you,
Maribeth?
Hannah: No, have they dug up something? There's
never any real answer. Was he a Lennon freak?
Jones: Yes, a great admirer of Lennon's. He somehow
confused himself, in his psychotic state, with being
John Lennon, and in his confusion the only thing that
kept him from fully being his idol was John Lennon the
man.
Hannah: My God. (Whistles).
Jones: That's what the psychiatrists are saying.
Hannah: Makes you afraid of being famous, doesn't it.
Jones: Yes. Is there any hope for Ray? What is his
hope at the end of the book? The only things he loves
and believes in are sex, poetry or art . . .
Hannah: And music. That last part is a dream you
know, like "Imagine," Lennon's song. Imagine. I don't
know if I did it right, but he goes into a dream state
there: "I hear a voice calling me and I'm not afraid."
It's a dawn. These are his wishes. Now Ray is an ideal-
ist, like many drunks. He wishes for the time in which
the war between men and women is over, "and we shall

stroll as naked Esalen couples under the eye of the sweet
Lord again." He really wants that. He has that dream
and wakes up and his wife hits him over the head with
a pillow, you know, she thinks he's thinking about
having relations with his nurse, which he might
have been on any other day. He has his idealism. I will
expect Ray, who may appear later, who knows, to
really be at war against his own sins and those of the—
anything that has confused and cheapened love. He
really does not like the American middle class. I think
he's going to be a constant warrior. And he may act.
He's a dangerous man, he really is. Just because he gets
straight or has a dream, that doesn't mean he has lost
his fury, you know?

Jones: Yes.

Hannah: There are enemies that should be known and
identified, who are polluted. He is never going to lose
hatred of that. What's that from Dylan, "Don't never
hate nothing but hatred." But you are never going to
find too many crusaders who're absolutely unblemished.
Martin Luther King had his private life. We ain't
Jesus. Why? Why is it that a person who is kind of
moral like me, why do I get in a rage when I see these
evangelists with their mansions that come on with their
wives that sing duets with them, the PTL? Is it because
I'm so nasty? How come it's younger people who don't
have my background at all that can see a phony like
that instantly? What's wrong? Is it me that just has
this detector, this odd detector? No. The more you read
about them the phonier you find they are. So Ray's rage
will go on.

Jones: So where do you go with the rage? Is that why
he went to the bottle?

Hannah: Partly. He said at one time he doesn't like
doctors. That's a category. He doesn't like doctors' children's revolt. On the other hand, you don't have to go
along with all brother Ray's hates. He is a bigot, you

know? He is a bigot. I don't know. As long as he is not
self-destructive and doesn't hurt anybody else he's a
good man, a good character to live with. I like to mess
with people as minor characters in other books sometimes that I've written about as, you know, just them.
So Ray might come to a party or something and they
might kick him out.

Jones: Might meet up with Harry Monroe, as Thorpe
Trove did.

Hannah: Yes, right. They are fun once you get a
group going. But I'm not dedicated to perpetuating
Ray as a model or prototype. That is a sweet book
though. There is an angrier book I wrote last year. I
don't know if I want to get it on or not. It may be too
personal. I don't know. I'm for love. I'm for good
marriages. And I do want to protect the innocent. Is
that enough?

Jones: Yes. Do you need to go?

Hannah: I'm not going anywhere.

Jones: Let me ask you a couple more questions before
we cut it off.

Hannah: Okay.

Jones: You say you started off with *Ray* at about 400
pages, and then you cut it down to these short scenes,
these two paragraph messages.

Hannah: Yes.

Jones: Was that a new form of fiction as you were
trying to explore it, or what?

Hannah: Yes. It's not a literary man writing it, although he wants to be literary very much. He wants to
write good poetry. But he is at the edge of madness
sometimes, you know? Some of those things are extremely short, but it's like they hit your mind and they
are gone. Sometimes almost irrelevant things. One time
it's the coordinates for shooting a missile coming as
numbers. But I think it might happen to an ex-jet
pilot, you know? Just sheer numbers. There's a guy in

California who's in love with numbers and codes, and sometimes even static. So I was trying to get that. If it was experimental that's what I was trying to get. And then sometimes rather longish reflections. But it breaks it up.

Jones: Yes. Certainly it's not in any conventional structure, and it's hard to find a plot line in there you can follow from start to finish.

Hannah: No. I'm overjoyed that some of the people who've read it and written about it can see that the plot, though not really plotted, there is a plot. It's a very simple plot: his friendship with the Hooches and Sister, his love affair with Sister, his wife, his new marriage, his rather shoddy practice, his ambitions as a poet, and that's about it. She gets murdered, his marriage goes to hell, and Mr. Hooch survives. That's about it, and it ain't too much. But it's there. But to enjoy the book and let it take you without conventional plot is the idea. I wanted it to be a page turner without the idea of a serial, you know, what comes next.

Jones: That's interesting. Do you plan to continue that mode, or was it just an experiment?

Hannah: No, I like it. Since I'm writing movies now I think it works awfully well with cinematic work. Obviously somebody out there likes it too. It's in simple English too. There are not many words in there you have to hustle to the dictionary for. It's accessible too. I like that too, because I am not a literati intellectual. I'm smart enough, but I don't want to push brightness. I hate people who push complexity, needless complexity. I'll stay with that a while, see what I can get out of it. So much can be done with the English sentence. It's just beautiful.

Jones: That's where I think you're great, honest. You make the language art in itself, and just by using the way people talk, the way we all talk.

Hannah: Thank you, thank you.

Jones: I mean it.

Hannah: You know, this sounds like an old freak talking about "those were the days." Actually I've been in situations where I've been persecuted a little bit for using the English language and taking care with what I say, you know, just talking; not the lingo of a lot of people I've met. You almost get cut down for giving a little . . .

Jones: Just an accurate word, a big word.

Hannah: Yes. I don't use them consciously to blow anybody over. But for just caring about what you say and making it kind of true maybe, and maybe a little eloquence, or a little better than usual. They don't like that. It makes them uncomfortable.

Jones: That's the truth.

Hannah: "Where does he get his airs?" It's like it's some unknown talent from the hills. (In bumpkin accent) "He's not one of us, Marge." You kind of make yourself into a freak, like I'll be down there in October at the Mississippi State Fairgrounds: "This man actually uses the English language!"

Jones: First in captivity!

Hannah: Yes. People avoid you, I'll tell you. Did you see that movie *The Elephant Man?*

Jones: Yes.

Hannah: That man was an eloquent speaker. It went along with the horror of his physique. He was so eloquent it made me cry, you know? I kind of like that, the elephant man, "Unveil him!"

Jones: In your fiction you've gone from a long 350 page *Geronimo Rex* to *Nightwatchmen* which was what? 220 pages?

Hannah: Something like that.

Jones: Down to the short stories of *Airships* to the novella of *Ray.* Why does the length continue to diminish in your work?

Hannah: Okay, I don't think I'm leaving out anything, for one thing. I'm still trying to pack enough reverb into the sentences that I write that I used to get by being long-winded. I'm shooting for that, and if I'm successful I'm delighted. But I'm not ignoring the possibility of a long book. Length means nothing to me as long as what is said is what should be said. So it is no concern at all. One of my favorite writers just wrote a monster: Anthony Burgess. It apparently is about everything. I've not read it. But he covers the waterfronts, doesn't he? Have you read some of it or all of it?

Jones: Just the review in the *New York Times. Earthly Powers.*

Hannah: And I understand *Sophie,* which is a monster, is worth reading. It's Styron's thing.

Jones: Yes, *Sophie's Choice.*

Hannah: *Sophie's Choice?* So it's just different strokes. I don't know. There are other long books I just don't think are worth it. I put them down, baby. *Something Happened,* did you ever get through that? Joseph Heller?

Jones: No.

Hannah: About that thick. My word! It's almost like a joke about how long you can be about zip, you know?

Jones: Yes. Was there anybody who influenced that laconic style of yours?

Hannah: I hate to deny something that could be so obviously true to everybody but me. It's funny. People who write short books: Donald Barthelme I admire, Vonnegut really packs it. I'm sure I got some influence from those boys. Beckett packs it. So, although I am not a sponge, they were around, and you can't deny it. Playwrights too can do it. A good playwright can really pack dialogue. Pinter. You know Pinter?

Jones: Sure, Harold Pinter.

Hannah: Yes. He doesn't have to gab. If you put some people in the right situation their words are just gold.

Jones: So, you're working on a screenplay right now?

Hannah: Yes, *The Big Jim Folsom Story.* I hope people
will remember him and the movie does go well. He is
another anomaly of Southern politics. A drunkard, but
you got to remember the guy is a guy too. You don't
say, or at least I don't anymore, "Well, that drunk." I
always wonder, "What kind of drunk? Does he beat his
wife? Or is he like some I know, sweet, sweeter than
his wife? I wish he'd beat her," you know? Or, "That
woman's a drunk," and I say, "Okay, hold it," and I go
meet her and she seems delightful. Maybe she has a
disease, but she is a gorgeous creature in all ways. Big
Jim had that curse, but remember he was an enormously out of kilter man: six feet eight whose wife died
while he was in the service, which I think would be a
blow to anybody to come back home to that in empty
Alabama. Then he kind of fell into politics. I ain't
going to tell you everything about it. It's well known if
you've ever read anything about Cornelia Wallace who's
his niece. They jabber all the pitiful stories about Big
Jim around, but he had his heart set apparently at least
once in the right place: he was for blacks, against the
Klan, for building roads for the farmer: "The Big Man
for the Little Man." He's not to be ashamed of. When
he should have been a Dixiecrat he was not.
Jones: '48.
Hannah: Yes. So, there he is, and I think it will make
a marvelous story. They were looking at Nick Nolte,
which I thought was awful. I didn't know the man
could act, but apparently he can. He's a big man, and
if he sweeps his hair back he might can do it.
Jones: Was Big Jim blond-headed?
Hannah: No. Little things. (In Hollywood director's
nasal tone) "Hey, you wanna get that brunette big
guy?"
Jones: Right. We've talked for about an hour or so,
Barry.
Hannah: All right.

Jones: But let me say for the tape how much I appreciate you sitting with me and sharing some of this. I enjoyed it.

Hannah: Well, thank you, John. I'm flattered, and I like to talk to intelligent people. It's not a chore at all.

Jones: I've been your fan for a long time. Thanks from the Archives, too.

Hannah: You're welcome.

Jones: Thank you too, Maribeth.

Kitchings: Oh, you're welcome.

Photograph by Christine Wilson

Beth Henley

ૐ

March 10, 1981

This interview was conducted about a month before Beth
won the Pulitzer Prize for her play, *Crimes of the Heart.*
At the time of our meeting, the play had been accepted
for the 1981 Broadway season, having just completed a
successful five-week run off-Broadway in December 1980
and January 1981. Our mothers are friends of long
standing, and it was through their combined efforts that
I secured the scripts of *Crimes of the Heart* and *The Miss
Firecracker Contest,* and then was able to interview Beth
during one of her brief visits to her childhood home in
Jackson. At twenty-eight, she was not inured to the
interview process. She sat in a high-backed chair with
one leg under her and spoke in an open and unself-
conscious way. On the Monday night in April when we
got the news that Beth had been awarded the Pulitzer
Prize there was great excitement and rejoicing in our
home.

Jones: This is John Jones with the Mississippi Department of Archives and History, and I'm about to interview Beth Henley. We are at Beth's mother's house.
This is where you grew up?

Henley: Well, after the fourth grade I moved here.

Jones: Right. It's a house on Avondale in Jackson, Mississippi. Today is Tuesday, March 10, 1981. As I told you before we cut the tape recorder on, Beth, I just wanted to get some basic biographical data first, if you could tell me something about your early life, when and where you were born, your schooling and things like that.

Henley: I was born in Jackson on May 8, 1952. I went to St. Andrew's Day School for the first through the third grade, and then I went to Duling Elementary School, and then I went to Bailey Junior High School.

Jones: Did you?

Henley: Yes, did you go there?

Jones: Yes.

Henley: I went to Murrah. That's all in Mississippi. Then I went to S.M.U. in Dallas for four years. Then I did one year of graduate work at the University of Illinois.

Jones: In what?

Henley: In acting.

Jones: Theatre arts, yes. Did you act all through high school? Were you in the Murrah players, or whatever?

Henley: No. I wasn't even in the Thespians. I'm surprised. When I look back now, most of my friends were in the Thespians, but I never was.

Jones: When did you get interested in it?

Henley: Well, I did some plays at New Stage. I went to a class that they had there. I can't remember if I was actually in a play there. Yes, I was. Oh, gosh. What's that one I did with John Maxwell?

Geno: I can't remember.

Henley: *Stop The World.*

Jones: Let me mention this: With Beth and me are Chrissy Wilson from the Department, and C. C. Geno, Beth's sister. You did this play when you were in college?

Henley: In high school.

Geno: And you were in *Summer and Smoke* when you were little.

Henley: Right. I did *Summer and Smoke* when I was in the fifth grade.

Jones: We'll talk more about that. Are your family roots in Hazlehurst and Brookhaven, the settings of *Crimes of the Heart* and *Miss Firecracker?*

Henley: Right. My mother's family is from Brookhaven and my father's family is from Hazlehurst.

Jones: I see. You still have family there now?

Henley: Yes, in both places. My grandmother still lives in Hazlehurst, and some of my cousins and an uncle, my father's brother and his wife. And then in Brookhaven, my mother's mother and some great-uncles and aunts and cousins, and an uncle lives there.

Jones: That's interesting. And you would visit there a lot when you were growing up, spend summers there and things?

Henley: We'd go down there a lot on the weekends, go down for the holidays.

Jones: So you went to S.M.U. for four years?

Henley: Right.

Jones: I have some newspaper clippings written about you, and in those articles I read that that was where you took your first playwriting course.

Henley: Yes.

Jones: Your last year?

Henley: No, it was my second year.

Jones: I'm interested to get you to describe by what process you finally decided to sit down and write. Had you been thinking about it your whole life?

Henley: No. I wanted to write, I think, when I was in junior high school, but then I started reading books and I said, "No way. I could never write." It was just too hard. I wasn't even that hot in English, in grammar and spelling and stuff. Then I took a playwriting course just like you take theatre history or lighting design. It was something I thought would be fun. You had to write a play to pass, so I wrote that play.

Jones: What play?

Henley: *Am I Blue* is the name of it. It's a one-act.

Jones: And that was your first try?

Henley: Well, in the sixth grade I wrote a play that we tried to produce. Other than that, I was in a creative writing course in junior high school, and I remember having to read my story in front of the class. I said, "But I'm not finished," and they said, "Ah, go on and read it anyway, 'cause nobody's written anything anyway." So I got up to read and I was about half-way finished and it wasn't sounding like I wanted it to sound like. I smashed it up and threw it in the trash and ran out of the class crying. Like I thought I was really going to get in trouble, but the teacher felt so sorry for me she didn't say anything.

Jones: So that was your first production.

Henley: Yes, in that creative writing class.

Jones: Was *Am I Blue* ever staged?

Henley: Yes. My senior year—I'd written it my sophomore year—my senior year they were doing Rick Bailey's play called *Badlands* at the time, I think he's changed it to *The Bridgehead,* and they needed a companion piece to go on the bill with it. Jill Peters was a director there, and she was looking through all the old one-acts that had been written and she found mine. She said, "This is the most together play I've come across, so why don't we do it?" So I did a few rewrites on it and they did it to fill out the evening.

Jones: Hm. Have you ever or have you yet tried prose or poetry? Is playwriting your only creative concern?

Henley: No, I haven't tried them yet. I don't know if I could do them. I used to write some poetry when I was a freshman. We'd all sit down and see who could write the grossest poetry, weird poems. But that's all I

did. I did that when I was a freshman. I still don't have
good grammar for putting like a whole novel or whole
story together. I can just write dialogue.

Jones: Do you think that's something you'd like to
try? Certainly you have the ear and the eye.

Henley: To write like a novel or something?

Jones: To write prose.

Henley: I might try that. It would be a relief because
once you finished it and somebody published it you
wouldn't have to worry about it anymore. With a play
that's where your problems just begin.

Jones: Yes. Tell me, after *Am I Blue* came, *Crimes of
the Heart* was your next one?

Henley: Well, I wrote the book for a musical my first
year after I was out of S.M.U. A friend of mine who's a
really talented musician wanted to write a musical, and
said, "I really like that play you wrote, so why don't
you write the book for this?" So I said okay. I was
working at horrible jobs all the next year after I
graduated. So I wrote the book for the musical at that
time, and the students did it right before I left for
Illinois. It was fun because I had never been around
musicians that much. It was a 1940s musical called
Parade. It was a real exciting thing to do.

Jones: What is the book?

Henley: The book. That's just the dialogue. There's a
composer and a lyricist. Somebody writes the music,
somebody writes the lyrics to the music, and I wrote
the lines the people actually say in between the songs.

Jones: Oh, yes. Tell me something·about the genesis
of *Crimes of the Heart.*

Henley: Okay. I was out in Los Angeles, I was trying
to act. It was so hard trying to get a job out there. I
had an acting agent, but she'd never call you up and I'd
sit at home all day long. She was reduced to working at
the Broadway Department Store and making calls on
her lunch hour. I was working with a group of actors

out there, among them Rick Bailey the playwright, and I thought I'd just write a play with parts for people around our age and we can do it as a showcase out there. I thought I may as well do something while I was sitting out there. I'd written a screenplay when I first got out there, so I was kind of in the habit of writing.

Jones: What happened to the screenplay?

Henley: The screenplay is called *The Moonwatcher*. It takes place in Illinois, which is from when I worked there, and it's about a girl who's kind of at a crisis in her life. She's been jilted by the boy that she's in love with. She's going to have his baby but he marries somebody else and she has to give up her baby. Now she's all confused. Now, just before I left Los Angeles to go to Dallas, there was a lady who'd read the screenplay and she really liked it and is interested in it, so I'm glad it didn't just die. I thought it was kind of dead. I don't know if anything will happen to it.

Jones: What's the difference in writing a screenplay and writing a play?

Henley: I don't know. That screenplay was really just one of those gifts, you know, just came to me image after image. It seems it was a lot easier to write than any play I ever wrote because you can just say something very quickly and very vividly and move on to something else. I really enjoyed writing it, but it's just so impossible. For two years after I wrote that I couldn't get anybody to read it, much less consider producing it—you know, millions of dollars. With a play you can feasibly do it on your own. At the time that was a consideration. I wanted something that could be done.

Jones: What years are we talking about when you were in L.A. and looking for work?

Henley: Okay. I left Illinois the fall of 1976 and moved to Los Angeles. Let's see. My play, *Crimes of the*

Heart, wasn't done in Louisville until 1979, so that's
that many years of destitution.

Jones: Goodness. What were you doing out there during this time, besides writing?

Henley: Working at temporary jobs that I hated, trying to avoid work.

Jones: Did you ever get any work as an actress?

Henley: No, I didn't, come to think of it. I worked in
a workshop, but I never got any work.

Jones: Out there with some people that you knew
from S.M.U. or from Illinois?

Henley: Yes, some people from Texas, some people
who were at S.M.U. ahead of me were out there.

Jones: When did you—I'm asking too many
chronological questions. It's like a history test. We'll
talk about the other in a minute. When did you decide
to sit down and write *Crimes of the Heart?*

Henley: Let's see. I wrote that in seventy . . . Daddy
died in 1978. That was right before I finished it. I
wrote it in 1978.

Jones: How long did it take you?

Henley: It only took me three months to write the first
draft. I had to do a lot of rewrites on it, a rewrite every
production. I had to do one rewrite before it went to
Louisville, and then one during rehearsals at Louisville,
and then for all the other productions I've worked on it.

Jones: Were these full-fledged rewrites or just cutting?

Henley: Just mainly cutting. Like the major cut I've
done is cut Uncle Watson out. I don't know if you have
a script with Uncle Watson in it. I had to cut him out
for the New York production. That's just like a page
and a half really. But, no, the characters have remained
the same. The end is what I've had to work on. It's
really pretty much intact. I've added some and sub-
tracted some.

Jones: Did it hurt your feelings when they asked you
to cut your play?

Henley: No. I was overly eager at first, because I was so happy to be having it done. I was just a slave to trying to please them. I was just the opposite. Now I'm not so much.

Jones: Now you have your own opinions about it.

Henley: Right.

Jones: Will you tell me why you sat down and wrote it, what inspired you?

Henley: You mean the idea?

Jones: Well, yes.

Henley: I kind of had two different ideas. One was based on my grandfather, my father's father, had gotten lost in the woods in Hazlehurst. They called up. I didn't go home. I was in Dallas at the time. For three days he was lost in the woods. They had picnic tables out there, and helicopters. In the Copiah County paper they had like, "Thirty foot snake found in the search for W. S. Henley!" And they had paratroopers. . .

Geno: The National Guard.

Henley: The National Guard. The governor came down. It was just a huge deal. People were out on horseback, people were out on foot.

Geno: The Coca-Cola people came in their trucks and advertised free cokes.

Henley: Did you go down there?

Geno: Yes.

Henley: Anyway, my grandfather was just walking through the woods, and according to him was never lost. He knew where he was: Copiah County. He found this little shack. He got to this little shack, and these people brought him into town and they got to a gas station where some people were saying. "They're gonna find that old man, but he'll be dead." And he said, "No they are not! Here I am alive!" So he returned alive after three days. So I thought that would be a good idea for a play: a family crisis bringing everybody back home. It was too close or something, anyway I couldn't get a lead on writing a play about my grandfather getting lost in the woods. I had that idea: a family and everybody gets back home. Also I heard this story about Walter Cronkite was sitting up on the front porch of these rich people's house in the South, and this little black kid came up and said he wanted ice cream, and the man came down and socked him in the face and said, "Don't you ever come around to this front door again." That made such an impression on him. I thought, "God, I'd like to kill somebody for just being cruel like that to some innocent person." So that kind of gave me the idea of Zackery beating up on Willie Jay. I thought it would be interesting to write about a character who tries to kill somebody, but you'd be in their corner rather than in against them. So I kind of combined those two ideas. I guess that's what started it.

Jones: You said you were hesitant to write about your grandfather being lost in the woods in Copiah County because it is too close to you. My question is how much of your writing is bits and pieces of what you have heard, your memory, and how much is imagination?

Henley: I don't know if I could say a percentage.

Jones: No.

Henley: But some of the things I might not have heard from my family but have heard from other people in Texas or even in New York that I transposed down to the South, to Mississippi; or even in Los Angeles because that's where I live now. But a lot of them are from stories I've really heard, more in *Miss Firecracker* than *Crimes of the Heart*. I totally made that up about being hung with the cat. I never knew anyone who would shoot their husband because they didn't like their looks, and then go fix lemonade. I made all that up. I don't really.

Jones: I know that's kind of a nebulous question. Chrissy and I were talking about that on the way over here. Are there things as a writer that you won't touch, that are too close? Do you feel that as a writer you are able to deal with any emotion of anybody, you can use any family history, that everything is open to you because you're an artist? Or are you shy about talking about certain things?

Henley: I think I would prefer to disguise certain things, you know, instead of . . . I've put some things in my plays and I wondered how people would react. Usually they don't even remember saying them or doing them or something like that. For some reason I don't like to get too factual, because it's too confining. It's easier for me to deal with that area of fiction where you're not stifled by having to adhere to "I'm going to write this story to really show how my father was, or my grandmother was."

Jones: Right.

Henley: I don't think I really answered your question. I guess if it's something really good I don't feel that bad about putting it in, you know. I'll just stick it in there. I don't think I've hurt anybody's feelings so far. People always like to read themselves into your work. When it was about three sisters my sisters assumed it was going to be about them and our lives and everything. They were kind of surprised when they saw it: "That's nothing like me!"

Jones: Right. How has your family treated your success as a playwright? Do they like your work?

Henley: Oh, they love it. My mother has come up for practically all my productions. C. C. came up to New York with her husband. My mother and her new husband came up to New York. My father was the only one who didn't like it. He died before I ever made any money. I hadn't done anything and he was like, "What are you doing? You should go back to secretarial school and learn to type faster."

Jones: Yes. Your father was a Mississippi state senator, Charles Henley.

Henley: Right. Charles Henley.
Jones: And he died in 1978?
Henley: Right.
Jones: Before *Crimes of the Heart.*
Henley: Right.
Jones: I want to ask you something just to get your reaction to it. We don't necessarily have to include this in the transcript. My mother was talking with your mom about your success, and they were kidding like they do, and your mom was saying that your new play *The Wake* was based on the death of your father and the fact that his family took a long time to bury him, which was a matter of great pain for her. They were joking, you know. Was—did you write it based on your experiences at that time?
Henley: It's not based on any actual experience that I had at that time, except for the experience. It was definitely based on that. We were thinking then, "Gosh, this would make a great play." It was so interminable! All the family was together, and there was all this tension and all these raw emotions. That makes for a good play, I think. You know, people have an excuse to drink and an excuse to scream and an excuse to act their fullest. I thought that would be a real good idea for a play. There's not tons of similarities—I would say there are no similarities between the actual thing here. It was much grimmer than my play. My play's a real comedy. Here it was just really a drag. Maybe if you were in the play you'd look at it as a drag. I don't know.
Jones: And the guy in the play actually dies from getting kicked in the head by a mule.
Henley: A cow.
Jones: Right. Well, when you finished *Crimes of the Heart,* did you know you had something there? Had you read extensively in the plays that have come out over the last ten years and knew that yours was something new in the art?

Henley: I remember I was at T.R.W. in the parts department, back there after I'd written it. I had taken off from work to try to finish it; you know, temporary work. I thought, "Oh, God, I'll probably be doing this till I'm eighty." I didn't know. I mainly read old things. I missed a lot of reading when I was young, so I like to read more classical stuff. I don't read tons of contemporary plays. I didn't really know what the score was. I didn't even know they weren't doing three-act plays anymore. They told me, "They're not doing three-act plays anymore," and I went "They're not? Wow! Back when I was reading plays they were doing them." So I was real surprised that people liked it as much as they did.

Jones: You showed it to friends first. I know the story of your friend sending it to Louisville to the 1979 competition. So what happened then? Did you immediately get an agent? What happened to it after it was recognized?

Henley: Well, we had a reading at my house. It was real fun and went well. Then a friend of mine who was at the reading, her agent was trying to start a literary department out in Los Angeles. My agent, Gilbert Parker, was coming in to visit. He didn't have any scripts to read, so my friend told her agent, "Well, give him this of my friend's. It's really good." So she gave it to her agent who gave it to Gilbert. This was before it was done in Louisville. I got in that night and there was a message on my phone machine to call him. I didn't even know who he was. I didn't know who his clients were. "Mark Medoff, now I know he's written something. Paul Zindel?" He thought I was brainless beyond belief. It was so embarrassing. He got off the phone and said, "How can she write such good plays and be so. . ." I don't know if he said, "ignorant." So then he was my agent. He's real nice. He's a good agent. He just liked it from reading it.

Jones: I've also read where you said you wrote the play

with the intention of playing the part of Babe in a production of it. Any truth in that?

Henley: That was in the production we were going to do. They had that publicity that I was going to give myself a part. I was kind of embarrassed by that statement. But I did have in mind with the cast we were going to have that I would play Babe. Now I'm so old I probably couldn't play Lenny. That is true.

Jones: Let me ask you this: people that I've talked to have said that acting and writing is really much the same insofar as you're under the spotlight and if it's good it sticks, is remembered. Being an actress, do you think it was any easier for you to write?

Henley: Being an actress really helped me writing plays particularly. It is the same for me in a sense. You just get into a character, and what that character wants, what are their greatest dreams, their greatest fears, what would they feel at this moment or in this scene, you can both determine. As a writer I can play a fifty-three-year-old man, or I can play a tall brunette woman, you know, as many characters as you want. The pleasure of writing is when you write, and the hell of it is to go into rehearsals. With acting your creative work is in rehearsals. It's more immediate.

Jones: Yes. In the reviews I read some critic likened Babe to a character out of Flannery O'Connor, Meg to a, I believe he says, a benign Tennessee Williams, and then Lenny from Chekhov. Are those people you've read, and did you do that consciously?

Henley: I hadn't read Flannery O'Connor. Like, in my first review in Louisville they compared me to her. I hadn't read her. Now I love her. I think she's great. I had read Tennessee Williams and Chekhov, and I think they're great. Now, what did you ask me?

Jones: If you drew that parallel consciously, or if that tradition meant anything to you when you sat down to write?

Henley: Chekhov and Shakespeare, of course, are my

favorite playwrights. Chekhov, I feel he influenced me more than anyone else, just with getting lots of people on stage. I don't do anything close to what he does with orchestration. That fascinates me. I also like how he doesn't judge people as much as just shows them in the comic and tragic parts of people. Everything's done with such ease, but it hits so deep. So I guess I've got to say he influenced me more than I guess anybody.

Jones: What about the literary tradition of Mississippi, certainly with fiction. A lot of the humor you use in the two plays I've read is taking that Gothic Southern heritage and turning it upside down, you know, with the mother who hangs her cat and then herself. Do you take that old Southern eccentricity as something you are trying to satirize? Are you really conscious of that?

Henley: Well, I didn't consciously like say that I was going to be like Southern Gothic or grotesque. I just write things that are interesting to me. I guess maybe that's just inbred in the South. You hear people tell stories, and somehow they are always more vivid and violent than the stories people tell out in Los Angeles. It's always so mellow.

Jones: Right. Do you think you would have been a playwright had you grown up—there's really no way to answer that—say in California? Is your real inspiration here in Mississippi?

Henley: I don't think I'd be writing the same type of plays, but I'm not saying California is devoid of inspiration. The poet Charles Bukowski writes very well about Los Angeles. The South just suits me better.

Jones: Can you write when you're here in Mississippi?

Henley: No. I can't even breathe. I get hay fever every time I come here.

Jones: You really can't write?

Henley: I can take a few notes or something like that, but there is no way I could sit down and write in my parents' house. It's so in-and-out, you know, and there's too much going on to sit down and write.

Jones: When you come to Mississippi do you go to Brookhaven and Hazlehurst and visit the people?

Henley: I go to Hazlehurst all the time. I was there Sunday. But I don't go to Brookhaven as often.

Jones: I wanted to get you to describe what inspires your characters, your characterizations. Is it the small Southern town that interests you so? Is it something else?

Henley: I don't know, because Jackson's not really that small a Southern town. It's the one I grew up in. It's not a large metropolis. I think it's that in a small Southern town there's not that much to detract from looking at characters. If you live in Los Angeles there's just so much going on that you can't write about it. But here things are small and Southern and insular, and you get a bird's-eye view of peoples' emotions. I don't know if that's a good answer.

Jones: It is. Will you always return to Mississippi in your writing?

Henley: I'm really not sure. My next play takes place in the South, in Jackson, if I ever get to writing on it. But I'm not sure if I'll ever be able to write about Los Angeles, or if that will interest me. I just don't know. I like to write about the South because you can get away with making things more poetic. The style can just be stronger. If I could figure it out I'm sure I could do it with any place, but I haven't.

Jones: You've been in New York for a while. Does the cultural world still think things Southern are neat?

Henley: I haven't really spent a lot of time in New York because my play only ran five weeks. I was there for the rehearsals and for a few days. There were no lines of people dying to find out about me by any means. I'm not really sure about New York because I was there for only a short time.

Jones: Your play is going to run on Broadway next season?

Henley: Right. In the fall.

Jones: Let me get you to talk to this too: John Simon said that the only fear he had was that your play *Crimes of the Heart* came from a stockpile of youthful memories, and that there was a chance—I know you remember his saying that—and that there was a chance that you would not be able to come up to what that play is ever again. What do you think about that?

Henley: Well, I was just glad I'd finished those two other plays by that time so I didn't panic and be in total distress. I don't think *Crimes of the Heart* was as autobiographical as he was implying. It's true I'm from Mississippi, and I have two sisters, but my mother isn't dead with suicide, my sister hasn't shot her husband, you know, my sister doesn't have a missing ovary. All the characters were imaginary. I guess it is biographical in the sense that they were sisters and they are from Mississippi.

Jones: He also said, or others have said, that it is a play about adversity being triumphed over by unity and a family coming together. I've read where you said that, and then said, "I guess that's the theme of the play, that's what they tell me." Was the play defined for you by the critics?

Henley: A lot of it really was. It's much easier for me to talk about it after reading my reviews. It was like, "Oh, I see, that's what it's about," because I don't think very thematically. I think more in terms of character and story. I don't necessarily know whether I'm writing it to any end, you know, to any theme. Like, I just found out vaguely what the theme to *The Wake* might be after we had the reading. I said, "I think I may know what this play's about." See, I didn't know when I was writing it, and watching it made it much more simple.

Jones: Yes. That's one of the reasons I was anxious to talk with you, especially after reading your quote about the theme of *Crimes of the Heart*. Many of the artists today are so concerned with art for art's sake, you know, having the right lingo when talking about"their art," that it's really great to be able to talk with someone young like you who has maybe not learned all the ropes, and maybe whose art is more spontaneous and real than the rest. You know what I mean? Is that helpful to what you are trying to do? I don't know how to make a question out of it.

Henley: Well, I think it's helpful not to be confined by anything at the start, you know, "This is what my play's going to be about." Well, maybe that's not what your play's going to be about, maybe you don't have the vaguest idea, maybe your characters want it to be about something else. Also, I don't like the idea of a playwright sitting there saying, "This is what my play's about," because then everybody says, "Well, if the playwright says this is what it's about then this is what it's got to be about." People can have different viewpoints about it. It can mean different things to different people. If you have it in black and white that that's what you're thinking about, you might not think that's what it's about if you read it ten years from now. So I really wouldn't like to write down what I think about the theme of my play.

Jones: What about *The Miss Firecracker Contest*, did that come quickly?

Henley: No, that was hard to write. I was doing a lot of traveling then. Before, I didn't have anything to distract me at all. When I was writing *Crimes* there was no pressure, you know. This was harder to write because I was having to go here and there. And *The Wake* was even harder. That's too bad.

Jones: You were writing *Miss Firecracker* during the Louisville time, or was it before that?

Henley: No, right when I got back from Louisville I started working on it. I worked for television that summer, so I had to do that for three months. Then in the meantime there had been a production in California of *Crimes*, and then there was a production in the fall of *Crimes* that I had to go to. That was in St. Louis. Gosh. Then I got to work on *Miss Firecracker*. Then I finished it, I think.

Jones: Was the Jackson New Stage production of it the first?

Henley: The second. It was done in Los Angeles at a ninety-seat showcase theatre, the Victory Theatre.

Jones: And where is it now?

Henley: It's in Dallas.

Jones: Right. So it came harder than *Crimes*, and *The Wake* was harder still?

Henley: Right. The next one will be impossible. Actually it's not as hard, it's just getting the time and getting your mind in the place of the play. When I get to work on another play my mind goes to work on that play. Then I have to get back and read over all my notes, and that's real boring but I have to do it so my mind will be on the play.

Jones: Did you have something, Chrissy?

Wilson: Yes. I just wanted to ask if you think New Yorkers can appreciate your plays as well as Southerners.

Henley: Oh, gosh. I think Southerners would have the edge generally speaking, but I think New Yorkers can enjoy the play. They have, but I do think maybe Southerners have an edge.

Wilson: You said earlier that your characters are not based on your family but maybe a caricature or exaggeration of many Southern families. When New Yorkers go to your play, do you think they think all Southern families are like that, or do you think a lot of Southern families are really like that?

Henley: I think a lot of Southern families are really like that. I heard people in the audience of *Crimes* say, "You know, my sister's just like that. That reminds me just of my sisters." They can relate to it like that. But I don't know.

Wilson: Better than New Yorkers can.

Henley: No, that is people from New York.

Wilson: They all think that.

Henley: Yes.

Jones: I've read where you said your next play will be about two old friends that meet in the restroom of the Stardust Ballroom during an Iggy Pop concert. That's your California play.

Henley: Yes. I've been trying to work that out in my brain.

Jones: Don't have anything down about it yet?

Henley: I have a few notes on it. I think that would be fun to write about. I could write about that, if I could just find the right tone to do it so it wouldn't be commenting on it or taking it lightly. You know, I'd like to make it real.

Jones: You would take it seriously?

Henley: Yes. You know, I've got to get to where I can understand the people enough to take them seriously and not make fun of them, figure out why they are doing that.

Jones: Why they are at an Iggy Pop concert with green hair.

Henley: Yes, why people become punkers.

Jones: I'd like to read that.

Henley: Yes.

Jones: Is that pretty much sweeping California? I know Steve, your boyfriend, is involved with a punk rock band.

Henley: Right. I don't know if he calls it punk rock, but I do. It's really a rock-and-roll band, the L.A. Slugs.

Jones: A good punk name.

Henley: Yes. They're real good.

Jones: Is he out there now?

Henley: No, he's here.

Jones: Yes, I've been seeing somebody wandering around. I thought that might be him.

Henley: Yes.

Jones: What about your success? I know it's changing your life, but is it changing the things you want to do? Will playwriting replace acting as your ambition?

Henley: Well, I would like to be able to do both. Like, I'm going to work in a play when I get back out to L.A. Writing is probably—it just gives you so much more freedom, because you can sit down there and you can create all this stuff and you don't have to worry about somebody writing a part that's right for you, casting other people that are good in it. You need so much to really make things work artistically as an actor. I mean, just getting cast at all is a miracle, much less in a part that you give a damn about. So I would like to write and just act in situations that I know would have some importance to me, rather than just beating my brains out to get a commercial.

Wilson: Beth, could you compare your satisfaction with the production here of *Miss Firecracker* and the Broadway production?

Henley: Well, they're two different plays.

Wilson: Yes, but I meant just as far as the quality of the production.

Henley: Well, I'll tell you, I was more satisfied with my production here with *Miss Firecracker* than I was with the one in New York. It's surprising. I really think it has a lot to do with having Southern actors in a play. It's such an edge they have to get in understanding these people that I just didn't see in the New York production—it was very Yankee stoic in many ways, instead of just bursting with the passion of these peo-

ple. I didn't like that at all. I worked to change it, and
it did improve. I just think on the whole that down
here was much more fun. The show was more my vision
than it actually ended up being in New York. The
structure was all fine in New York. It just lacked some
of the blood.

Jones: Is it hard as a playwright working with directors to get your vision across?

Henley: It's real hard. It really is.

Jones: You being young and female I was wondering if
you'd gotten any condescension.

Henley: Oh, yes! I think anyone would get condescension from directors. So many of them are so insecure. I
never realized it, but their jobs are really in jeopardy all
the time. The producers can fire them. It's harder to
get a job as a director than as an actor. They've got all
sorts of responsibilities. I've had generally good relations with the directors. But if you get on their bad
side then you better forget it. They won't listen to
anything you say, because they don't have to. I never
have had power enough to get a director fired, because
usually the director is more of a name than me, or is
the producer. I try to get along with them, and hope-
fully be with the director long enough so that we'll
have a similar vision of the play.

Wilson: Do you have a say in the casting?

Henley: In New York I did. I did here as a matter of
fact.

Jones: What are you going to have to do about the
Broadway production, are you cutting it again?

Henley: I'm making just a few changes. Probably people who saw it wouldn't even notice them.

Jones: Are you going up there for the casting? Or have
they done that?

Henley: They haven't cast it. They are trying to get
the same three women who did it at the Manhattan
Theatre, which would be good because they really are a

good ensemble. I mean, regardless of what I said before, they worked well together. And they got good reviews, and nobody wants to tamper with success, especially if the producer really wants to go for the bucks. But they may have other engagements, and you can't book an actor this far in advance according to the rules of Equity. So, we'll have to wait and see if they will accept it again.

Jones: So, is L.A. your permanent home now?

Henley: Gosh, I still can't relate to it. I have a Mississippi driver's license, Texas license plates and Illinois car insurance. I refuse to say L.A.'s my home. I can't believe it! But now I think I'd rather live in Los Angeles than New York, just because I have a house with a garden and a car you can drive. I don't know. I guess it is, for a while.

Jones: What about someone like Miss Welty who writes very movingly about us and lives down the road? Do you think you'll ever be able to do that?

Henley: I don't know. I may. Right now there's just too much I want to do besides just come back and live here. It would just be too quiet for me.

Jones: It's not too interesting right now to you.

Henley: No, that's not true. It is. I've just got friends in Los Angeles, and it would just be hard to leave. Steve works out there.

Jones: Well, You have anything else, Chrissy? C. C., you have anything else?

Geno: No.

Jones: This has been nice. I appreciate your having us over and talking with us. It's been really interesting.

Henley: God. How did it compare with all those other guys? They're probably really eloquent.

Jones: No, it's perfect. That's why I wanted to talk to you. You are the authentic thing, a real creative talent. Thanks again.

A second volume in this series will contain
interviews with Margaret Walker, Walker Percy,
Ellen Douglas, Turner Cassity,
Willie Morris, and James Whitehead.